The Nazis' Nuremberg Rallies

The Nazis' Nuremberg Rallies

JAMES WILSON

Pen & Sword
MILITARY

First published in Great Britain in 2012
and republished in this format in 2023 by
PEN & SWORD MILITARY
an imprint of
Pen & Sword Books Limited
Yorkshire – Philadelphia

Copyright © James Wilson, 2012, 2023

ISBN: 978-1-39907-788-0

The right of James Wilson to be identified as Author
of this Work has been asserted by him in accordance
with the Copyright, Designs and Patents Act 1988.

A CIP catalogue record for this book is available from the British Library

All rights reserved. No part of this book may be reproduced or transmitted in
any form or by any means, electronic or mechanical including photocopying,
recording or by any information storage and retrieval system, without
permission from the Publisher in writing.

Typeset in Optima by Chic Media Ltd
Printed and bound in the UK by CPI Group (UK) Ltd, Croydon, CR0 4YY

Pen & Sword Books Limited incorporates the imprints of After the Battle, Atlas, Archaeology, Aviation, Discovery, Family History, Fiction, History, Maritime, Military, Military Classics, Politics, Select, Transport, True Crime, Air World, Frontline Publishing, Leo Cooper, Remember When, Seaforth Publishing, The Praetorian Press, Wharncliffe Local History, Wharncliffe Transport, Wharncliffe True Crime and White Owl.

For a complete list of Pen & Sword titles please contact

PEN & SWORD BOOKS LIMITED
47 Church Street, Barnsley, South Yorkshire, S70 2AS, England
E-mail: enquiries@pen-and-sword.co.uk
Website: www.pen-and-sword.co.uk
or
PEN AND SWORD BOOKS
1950 Lawrence Road, Havertown, PA 19083, USA
E-mail: uspen-and-sword@casematepublishers.com
Website: www.penandswordbooks.com

Contents

Foreword 8
Introduction 9
Propaganda Postcards 18
Author's Comment 21

    Images from the Early Days 22
    Reichsparteitag 1933 25
    Reichsparteitag 1934 40
    Reichsparteitag 1935 61
    Reichsparteitag 1936 80
    Reichsparteitag 1937 95
    Reichsparteitag 1938 112
    Reichsparteitag 1939 133

THE NAZI LEADERS
    Martin Bormann 138
    Joseph Goebbels 140
    Hermann Göring 143
    Rudolf Hess 146
    Heinrich Himmler 149
    Adolf Hitler 151
    Baldur von Schirach 155
    Albert Speer 156
    Julius Streicher 159

Acknowledgements 163
Bibliography 163
Appendix 164

Alt Nürnberg

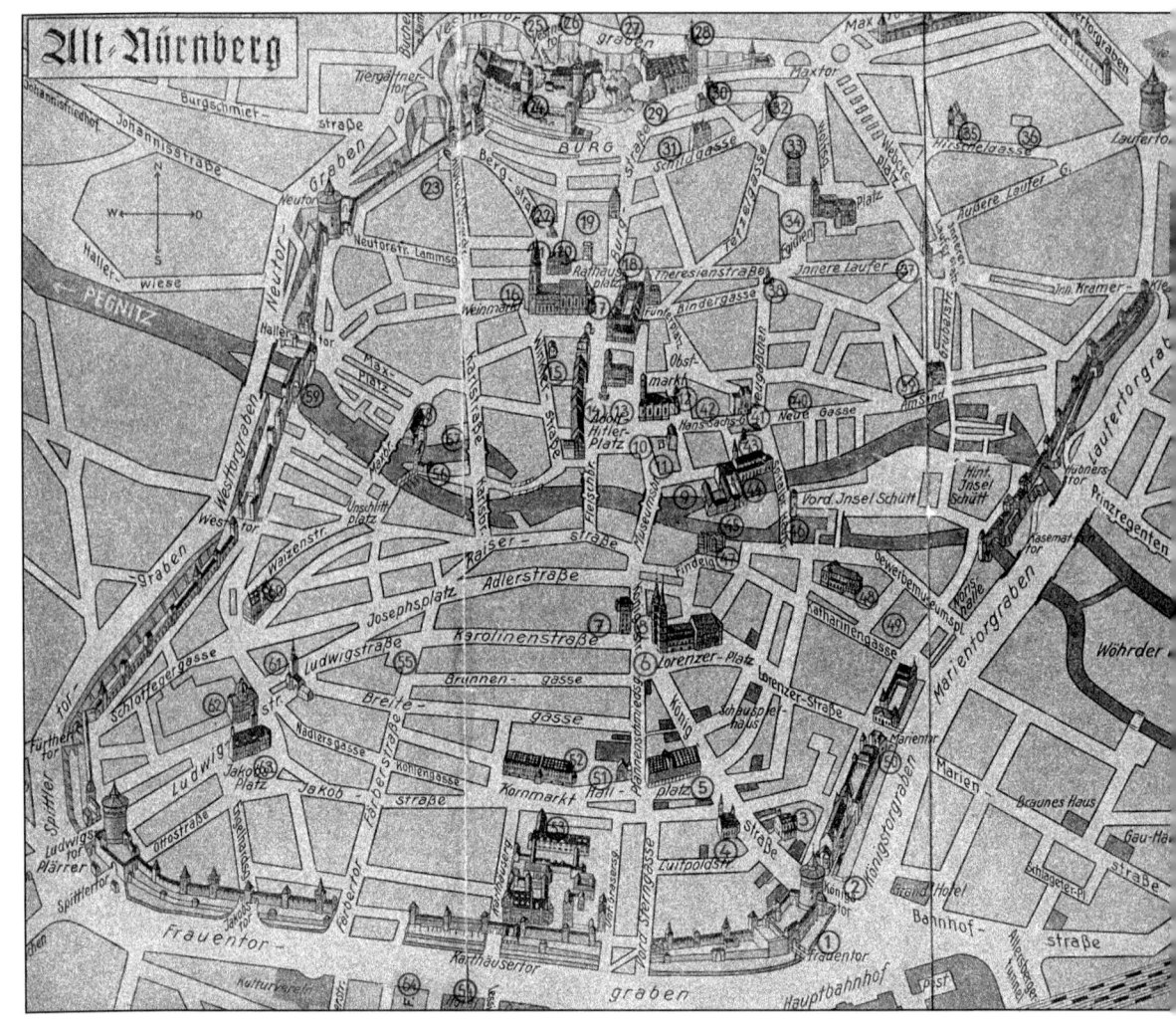

1 Frauentor
2 Künstlerhaus mit Städt Galerie
3 Marthakirche
4 Klarakirche
5 Mauthalle m. Städt. Mautkeller
6 Lorenzkirche
7 Nassauer-Haus
8 Tugendbrunnen
9 Heilig-Geist-Spital
10 Plobenhof (Schöner alter Hof)
11 Bratwurstherzle (Herzgasse)
12 Gänsemännchenbrunner
13 Frauenkirche
14 Schöner Brunnen
15 Musikhistorisches Museum
16 Sebalduskirche
17 Rathaus mit Rathaussaal und Lochgefängnissen
18 Stadtbibliothek, ehemals Dominikanerkloster
19 Fembohaus
20 Goldenes Posthorn älteste deutsche Weinstube
21 Moritzkapelle, Bratwurstglöcklein
22 Albrecht-Dürer-Denkmal
23 Albrecht-Dürer-Haus
24 Kaiserburg
25 Heidenturm
26 Sinnwellturm
27 Fünfeckiger Turm
28 Kaiserstallung
29 Luginsland
30 Toplerhaus
31 Haus zum goldenen Schild
32 Grolandhaus
33 Pellerhaus
34 Egidienkirche Melanchtondenkmal
35 Tucherschlößchen
36 Hirschvogelsaal
37 Laufer Schlagturm
38 Martin-Behaim-Denkmal
39 Hennenscheißhaus
40 Historischer Hof (Sehensw. Hof)
41 Dudelsackpfeifferbrunnen
42 Hans-Sachs-Haus
43 Hans-Sachs-Denkmal
44 Spitalkirche zum hl. Geist
45 Heilig-Geist-Spital
46 Schuldturm
47 Hindenburg-Hochschule
48 Katharinenkloster mit Reichskleinodien (Meistersingerkirche)
49 Bayer. Landesgewerbe-Anstalt
50 Fränkische Galerie
51 Zeughaus
52 Hopfenhalle
53 Germanisches Nationalmuseum
54 Hotel des Führers
55 Peter-Henlein-Brunnen
56 Henkersteg
57 Bayer. Hof (Schöner Hof)
58 Weinstadel
59 Kettensteg
60 ehemaliges Waizenbräuhaus
61 Weißer Turm
62 Elisabethenkirche
63 Jakobskirche
64 Gauwaltung DAF. und KdF.

Key to buildings

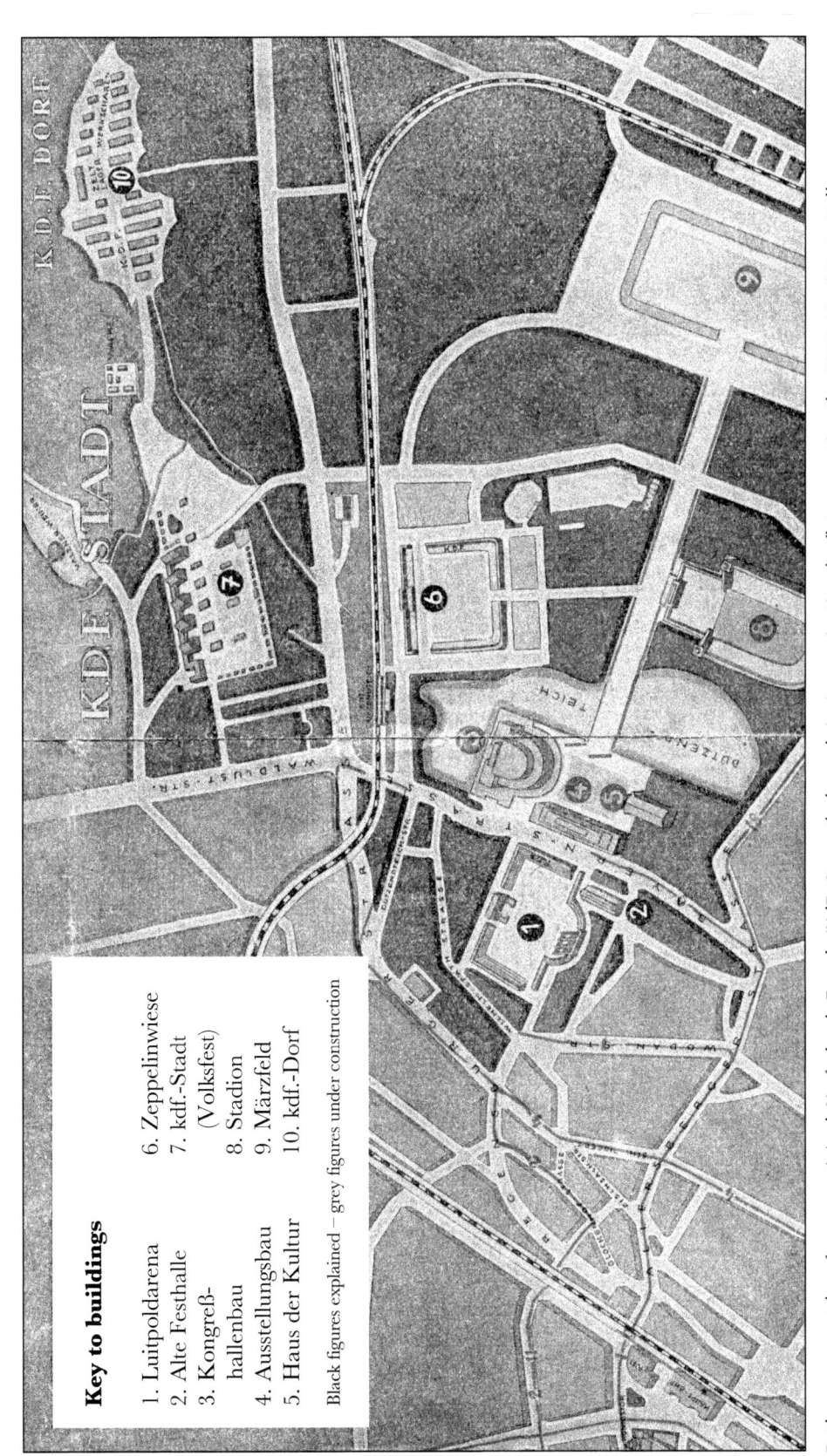

1. Luitpoldarena
2. Alte Festhalle
3. Kongreß-hallenbau
4. Ausstellungsbau
5. Haus der Kultur
6. Zeppelinwiese
7. kdf.-Stadt (Volksfest)
8. Stadion
9. Märzfeld
10. kdf.-Dorf

Black figures explained – grey figures under construction

Both maps are taken from an original *Kraft durch Freude* (KdF; Strength through Joy) organization leaflet promoting the 1938 Nazi Party Rally.

Foreword

Mankind's history is long and varied. Since ancient times man has felt the urge to reproduce images of the things that influenced his life. From the earliest cave paintings to the current digital age, man's almost inbred desire to record significant events, whether on a cave wall, on canvas, on film, or through those more recently developed electronic formats has remained undiminished through the ages. Prior to the introduction of photography in the nineteenth century the visual recording of an event of major significance was generally carried out by artists working on canvas, sometimes long after the event, and then often reliant on the memories or written records of others. This meant that accuracy, almost without exception, was questionable to say the least.

In so far as time itself is concerned, every passing second is confined to history, every moment gone forever never to be restored. With that in mind, when we consider the amount of time that has passed since man's first attempt to record meaningful events on a cave wall, in relative terms one might say that the Third Reich existed merely moments ago. To say that the Nazis felt the need to visually record their moment in history would be an understatement almost without equal. Hitler's Third Reich, unlike any other regime that existed before it, and indeed many that have followed, leaves the viewer quite breathless at the amount of photographic material produced during the brief twelve years and four months of its existence.

To what extent imagery enhances the communication of a story cannot be easily judged. However, it has been said that a story without pictures is only half the story. In this instance it is the imagery of the Third Reich that is used to communicate and enhance the reader's understanding of those major events in recent history known as the Nuremberg Rallies. Every image is as it were a small window into the past, a visual record of an event of major historical significance that the skilled photographers of the 1930s can still share with us today some eighty years later.

Introduction

The first NSDAP; *Nationalsozialistische Deutsche Arbeiterpartei* (National Socialist German Workers' Party) rally took place in *München* (Munich) in January 1923. Adolf Hitler, for his part in the failed Munich Beer-Hall *Putsch* (Revolt) that took place on 9 November 1923, was later found guilty of treason and spent the greater part of the year 1924 in Landsberg Prison. Thus no rally was held in 1924. One of the conditions of Hitler's early release on 20 December 1924 was a ban on public speaking, again no rally was held in 1925. In July 1926 the rally was held in Weimar. The following year, 1927, saw the rally held in the ancient city of *Nürnberg* (Nuremberg) for the first time.

These early 'rallies' were small, poorly organized events when compared to the later stage-managed, massed rallies of the 1930s. Often as not these early events ended in running street-battles with rival political groups. In creating the SA *Sturmabteilung* (Storm Detachment/Storm Troopers) in November 1921, Hitler, essentially, provided the Party leadership and its members with their first real means of protection. Following the success of the 1927 rally, it was decided that all future *Reichsparteitage* (National Party Days) would be held in Nuremberg.

> *'All great movements are popular movements. They are the volcanic eruptions of human passions and emotions, stirred into activity by the ruthless Goddess of Desire or by the torch of the spoken word cast into the midst of the people.'*
> – Hitler

During the early years of political ambition, and even when having secured his position as leader of the newly renamed NSDAP in July 1921, Adolf Hitler remained a driven man, an individual with a hunger for power that could hardly be satisfied. This situation continued through the early years of struggle, firstly, to achieve total control of the Party, then later to secure the office of Chancellor, then that of President, and finally that of Commander in Chief of the Armed Forces. While in so many ways a complex personality, there was a side to Hitler's character that always compelled him to try to bend every situation to his own will.

The manifest power of an event such as *Reichsparteitag* combined with the magnetic personality and compelling oratory of Adolf Hitler, proved an irresistible force to many otherwise, fair-minded, reasonable individuals. The Nazis, better than any other political movement before, or since, certainly knew how to work their audience. The fact that millions of people eventually fell under his spell and came to see Hitler as the saviour of Germany, chiefly through the influence of his oratory and a relentless propaganda campaign, bears testimony to this. His rousing and inflammatory speeches reveal an unrivalled mastery of propaganda.

In addition to his gift as a great orator, Adolf Hitler was an exceptionally skilled politician. He could see political opportunities where others could not and turn these to his advantage in a way that left his political rivals' heads spinning. Furthermore, he had an excellent memory. Hitler could read lengthy material relating to technical information and be able to recall that information accurately years later. But, and perhaps most important of all, was Hitler's ability to adapt himself to the audience he was facing in any given situation.

> 'The spark of a genius exists in the brain of the truly creative man from the hour of his birth. True genius is always inborn and never cultivated, let alone learned.'
> – Hitler

As a platform for the Nazi Party to woo and impress the many thousands of onlookers, the annual *Reichsparteitage,* later referred to as the Nuremberg Rallies, provided excellent opportunities for the Party leadership to expound their successes, but perhaps more importantly, they presented Adolf Hitler further opportunities to cement his relationship with the German people. Nuremberg had been carefully and deliberately chosen as the venue for the *Reichsparteitage,* not only because of its relatively central position and excellent transport links, but also because the city and its police force were sympathetic to the Nazi cause. Additionally, Nuremberg's Luitpoldhain provided adequate space for large outdoor events.

Furthermore, the Party could rely on Julius Streicher, Nazi *Gauleiter* (District Leader) in Franconia with headquarters in the city. As *Gauleiter,* the fanatically loyal Streicher controlled a large number of equally loyal Party members in the region. Nuremberg would become to Nazi Germany what the city of Rome had been to the ancient Roman Empire; to all intents and purposes Nuremberg was the spiritual home of the Nazi Party between 1927 and 1945.

Finally, there were additional sentimental and patriotic reasons for choosing Nuremberg, this medieval city steeped in German history. For many centuries Nuremberg had been referred to as the 'unofficial capital' of the Holy Roman Empire. This was the medieval city where the Imperial Regalia had been kept since 1423. The regalia never left the city's castle, other than when required for the coronation of a new emperor at a special ceremony in Rome. In 1796 however, the threat posed by the advancing French Army forced the removal of the regalia, first to Regensburg, for four years, then on to Vienna where it would remain. Additionally, the city's importance was marked by the fact that every newly-crowned emperor had been required to hold his first diet in Nuremberg. These diets formed an important part of the administrative side of the empire. Furthermore, the royal courts met at Nuremberg Castle.

Adolf Hitler was fully aware of the significance of Nuremberg, and its place in German history. Within days of the annexation of Austria to the German Reich on 12 March 1938, Hitler would have the Imperial Regalia returned to Nuremberg; the city which he himself described as 'the most German of German cities.'

> 'The broad masses of a population are more amenable to the appeal of rhetoric than to any other force.' – Hitler

The largest and most impressive *Reichsparteitage* were undoubtedly those that were held in Nuremberg between 1933 and 1938. Totally mesmerising, these awe-inspiring events captured the imagination of not only the German onlookers, they attracted much international attention. Organized with typical German efficiency, the vast crowds were treated to an audio/visual spectacular, where seemingly endless columns of SA and SS men marched through the city accompanied by military bands. Of course no

Reichsparteitag would be complete without the inevitable speeches; while night-time brought about the mysterious, almost pagan-like, atmospheric torchlight processions. As intended, the end result was a successful coming together and a strengthening of the bond between the Party and the people; but more than that, it was the encouragement with ever-increasing success of developing the idea of the Hitler cult.

> *'All propaganda has to be popular and has to accommodate itself to the comprehension of the least intelligent of those whom it seeks to reach.'* – Hitler

While promoting the ideals and strength of the Nazi Party to audiences drawn from all over Germany, the tremendous recruitment opportunities presented by these *Reichsparteitage* were not overlooked. Having witnessed the massed ranks of the SA, the SS, the RAD *Reichsarbeitsdienst* (State Labour Service) and the *Hitler Jugend* (Hitler Youth) parading through the city, many thousands were recruited to the Party, the SA, the SS (if the required standards were met) and other state organizations. With overtones approaching that of religious events, the Nuremberg Rallies reached their audience in a way that today seems almost impossible. The invasive, intrusive, compelling influence of the Nazi Party and that of its dominating, all-persuasive leader, Adolf Hitler, should never be underestimated.

> *'There must be no majority decisions, but only responsible persons, and the word 'council' must be restored to its original meaning. Surely every man will have advisers by his side, but the decision will be made by one man.'* – Hitler

The 1934 *Reichsparteitag* attracted over a million people. At Hitler's request, the event was captured on film by Germany's then most successful female film director, the innovative and much admired, Leni Riefenstahl. Her film, *'Triumph des Willens'* (Triumph of the Will) proved a breath-taking, spectacular portrayal of the Rally, and a technical masterpiece for the time. Triumph of the Will went on to achieve great acclaim winning a gold medal for artistry at the World Exhibition in Paris in 1937. Even today, and given the subject matter, the work is still considered to be the best political documentary film of all time.

Riefenstahl had to deal with many technical difficulties during filming; nonetheless, the end result was everything she had set out to achieve. Hitler, on viewing the film, was impressed and delighted with Riefenstahl's efforts. For him, the film captured the very essence of *Reichsparteitag*. While confirming Nuremberg's position as the Party's spiritual capital, the work also successfully communicated all the ritualistic pomp and ceremony of the entire event, with him, (Hitler), centre stage, portrayed as the supreme, all-powerful figure with all responsibility.

> *'The German people have become strong again in spirit, strong in will, strong in endurance, strong to bear all sacrifices.'* – Hitler

Albert Speer, Hitler's favourite architect, later friend and confidant, would play an important part in organizing and developing the *Parteitag-Gelände* (Party Day Rally Grounds) at Nuremberg. The buildings around the Zeppelin Field Arena were constructed under Speer's supervision between 1934 and 1937. The Führer's intention, with Speer's help, was to construct buildings that would stand for a thousand years. These great monuments of the 'New Order', eventually covering an area of approximately eleven square kilometres, would mirror those great monuments of past civilizations. Buildings like the Coliseum in Rome and the Acropolis in Athens would be dwarfed by those constructed at Nuremberg.

The 1934 *Reichsparteitag* afforded Speer an opportunity to reveal his genius for the theatrical. Having procured 130 anti-aircraft searchlights, Speer positioned the lights at regular intervals in a huge circle around the perimeter of the rally grounds. Upon being switched on, these searchlights, having been aimed directly up into the night sky, created what Speer called his 'Cathedral of Light' effect. The result was truly mesmerising and visible for miles around, a spectacular scene where columns of light rose thousands of feet into the darkness. Speer's innovation certainly impressed all those attending the Rally.

> 'Do you now appreciate the depth of our National Socialist Movement? Can there be anything greater and more all comprehending? Those who see in National Socialism nothing more than a political movement know scarcely anything of it. It is more even than religion; it is the will to create mankind anew.' – Hitler

Each *Reichsparteitag* was organized around a particular theme; the Party deliberately creating a programme structured around then current national and international events.

The 1st National Party Rally was held in Munich in January 1923.
(A second rally was held in Nuremberg in September 1923 with the theme; **'German Day Rally'**).

The 2nd National Party Rally was held in Weimar in July 1926 with the theme; **'Refounding Congress'**.

The 3rd National Party Rally was held in Nuremberg in August 1927 with the theme; **'Day of Awakening'**.
The short film entitled; *'Eine Symphonie des Kampfwillens'* (A Symphony of the Will to Fight) with a running time of about thirty minutes recorded the event. This film, when compared to those produced during the 1930s, comes across as quite amateur.

The 4th National Party Rally was held in Nuremberg in August 1929 with the theme; **'Day of Composure'**.
The film; *'Nürnberger Parteitag des NSDAP'* (The Nuremberg Party Day of the NSDAP) with a running time of about one hour recorded the event. Directed by Baldur von Schirach, this is a much better film than that made during the 1927 rally. Many of the elements found in the later films covering the mass rallies of the 1930s are already evident here.

The 5th National Party Rally was held in Nuremberg in September 1933 with the theme; **'Rally of Victory'**.
This rally celebrated Hitler and the Nazi Party's coming to power in Germany in January 1933.

Thereafter all *Reichsparteitage* in Nuremberg were held during the month of September.

The 6th National Party Rally took place in 1934 with the theme; **'Rally of Unity and Strength'**.

This rally produced the documentary film *'Triumph des Willens'* (Triumph of the Will) by Leni Riefenstahl.

The 7th National Party Rally took place in 1935 with the theme; **'Rally of Freedom'**.
The theme referred to Germany's then virtual abandonment of the Versailles Treaty.

The 8th National Party Rally took place in 1936 with the theme; **'Rally of Honour'**.
The theme referred to Germany's then recent re-occupation of the demilitarized Rhineland.

The 9th National Party Rally took place in 1937 with the theme; **'Rally of Labour'**.
The theme referred to the dramatic reduction of unemployment across Germany since the rise to power.

The 10th National Party Rally took place in 1938 with the theme; **'Rally of Greater Germany'**.
The theme referred to the recent annexation of Austria to the German Reich on 12 March 1938.

The 11th National Party Rally planned to take place in 1939 with the theme; **'Rally of Peace'** was cancelled; Germany invaded Poland on 1 September 1939.

The Nuremberg Rallies, particularly those staged between 1933 and 1938 were undoubtedly the high points in the annual Nazi calendar of events. The Nazi Party introduced a calculated new form of blanket advertising, the like of which was previously unknown, to impart the ideals of the Party to the masses quickly and efficiently. The Party promoted itself as representing progress and the future, while Hitler was presented as Germany's messiah. The unsuspecting public for their part, having never previously been subjected to such methods of intense propaganda and associated advertising and promotion, were beguiled and entranced.

Adolf Hitler believed that destiny had chosen him for his great task; to regain those territories lost after 1918 and to restore German national pride. That Hitler was a great orator cannot be denied. It has been stated by those who heard Hitler deliver an address, that each individual in attendance believed he was speaking to them personally, no matter how large the audience.

> *'The German people are not a warlike nation. It is a soldierly one, which means it does not want war, but does not fear it. It loves peace but also loves its honour and freedom.'* – Hitler

For all their flag-waving, firework displays, marching columns and rousing military music, the high point of every *Reichsparteitag* was, of course, the speeches, particularly those given by Hitler. Having made his ubiquitous dramatic entrance, the Führer would mount the stage and deliver an address lasting perhaps as long as two hours; an incredible amount of time to speak without interruption by any standard. Then, hoarse, bathed in sweat and exhausted, having captured his audience and led them through a whole spectrum of emotions he left the stage a spent force. During the course of any given *Reichsparteitag* Hitler would address many different groups representative of the different organizations within the Party, nonetheless, while certain elements of his speech were the same, much of the content was deliberately tailored to meet the needs and expectations of that specific audience.

'Through clever and constant application of propaganda, people can be made to see paradise as hell, and also the other way round, to consider the most wretched sort of life as paradise.' – Hitler

Highly organized and well orchestrated mass-media events, the Nuremberg Rallies deliberately targeted the onlookers. The resulting effect was something approaching mass hysteria, leading to a kind of conscious surrender of one's self through the massive display of almost total power emanating from the Party, but in particular that of its leader, Adolf Hitler. The lives of most of the observers of these spectacular events, even those non Party members, were irrevocably changed, perhaps forever. Albeit on a much smaller scale, a modern day rock concert might be used to provide comparisons with the levels of hysteria and enthusiasm generated at the Nuremberg Rallies of the 1930s.

'After fifteen years of work I have achieved, as a common German soldier and merely with my fanatical will-power, the unity of the German nation, and have freed it from the death sentence of Versailles.' – Hitler

Ritual was very much part of the Nazi mindset. This is clearly illustrated in one of their most solemn rituals; that of the consecration of new Party flags, an important event that always took place at Nuremberg. The *Blutfahne* (Blood Banner) acquired its name by having been drenched in the blood of the Nazi martyrs who had died during the failed Beer-Hall *Putsch* (Revolt) in Munich on 9 November 1923. This solemn, bordering on a religious ritual was carried out by Hitler, who, whilst holding a corner of the bullet-holed *Blutfahne* in one hand, would grasp the new flag with his other hand and touch it against the *Blutfahne*. Thus the new banner was 'sanctified' and imbued with the spirit of those whose blood had been spilled on the streets of Munich in 1923.

The revered *Blutfahne* made its last public appearance on 18 October 1944 at the Induction Ceremony of the *'Volkssturm'* (People's Army), an organization similar to Britain's 'Home Guard'. The *Volkssturm* was to be Germany's final line of defence in the face of the advancing Russians. What became of the *Blutfahne* at the end of the Second World War is unknown.

'I use emotion for the many and reserve reason for the few'. – Hitler

Heinrich Hoffmann, Hitler's personal photographer attended the Nuremberg Rallies to photograph the Führer and other members of the Nazi hierarchy attending these events. His work brilliantly captured the atmosphere of the *Reichsparteitage*. Hoffmann images appeared in newspapers, magazines, in poster form, and in books specifically dedicated to the Rallies. Highly developed Nazi propaganda, always aware of the value of strong imagery, also reproduced Hoffmann's work in postcard form. Cheap to produce and widely distributed, the photographic postcard proved a powerful vehicle in bringing the pomp and ceremony of the Nuremberg Rallies to all corners of the Reich. Hoffmann joined the Party in 1920 and almost immediately secured what would become an extremely lucrative position, that of personal photographer to Adolf Hitler. In 1929 the Führer would be introduced to a young photographic assistant working in Hoffmann's Munich studio, that assistant, was Eva Braun.

'Obstacles do not exist to be surrendered to, only to be broken.' – Hitler

Adolf Hitler was the first politician of the twentieth century to embrace air travel. During numerous political campaigning tours, and prior to coming to power in 1933, Hitler, unlike his political contemporaries was seen all over Germany, speaking at venues many miles apart in a single day and all thanks to the advantages afforded by air travel. Being seen and heard by people at different venues across the country, and all within a short space of time, paid dividends. Such methods brought Hitler directly and, perhaps more importantly, personally to the people. While the Nazi leader's political rivals failed to understand such innovation; it would cost them dearly.

> *'The doom of a nation can be averted only by a storm of flowing passion, but only those who are passionate themselves can arouse passion in others.'* – Hitler

The Nazi's innovative form of political campaigning challenged the old order. As for the unsuspecting masses subjected to these unprecedented, innovative propaganda techniques, many were drawn to the Party and soon gave their support. Nazi propaganda proved so intense, and so well directed, that it eventually permeated virtually all aspects of not only public life, but perhaps more importantly the private life of the individual. While they would not admit it, many of the techniques used by the Nazis have found their way into the modern day politician's bag of tricks – if in a somewhat diluted form.

> *'Struggle is the father of all things. It is not by the principles of humanity that man lives or is able to preserve himself above the animal world, but solely by means of the most brutal struggle. If you do not fight, life will never be won!'* – Hitler

Otto Strasser (1897-1974) leader of the NSDAP in the 1920s, later one of Hitler's harshest critics, wrote of Hitler:

> *'Hitler responds to the vibration of the human heart with the delicacy of a seismograph, or perhaps of a wireless receiving set, enabling him, with a certainty with which no conscious gift could endow him, to act as a loudspeaker proclaiming the most secret desires, the least admissible instincts, the sufferings and personal revolts of a whole nation. I have been asked many times what is the secret of Hitler's extraordinary power as a speaker. I can only attribute it to his uncanny intuition, which infallibly diagnoses the ills from which his audience is suffering. If he tries to bolster up his argument with theories or quotations from books he has only imperfectly understood, he scarcely rises above a very poor mediocrity. But let him throw away his crutches and step out boldly, speaking as the spirit moves him, and he is promptly transformed into one of the greatest speakers of the century. Adolf Hitler enters a hall. He sniffs the air. For a minute he gropes, feels his way, senses the atmosphere. Suddenly he bursts forth. His words go like an arrow to their target, he touches each private wound on the raw, liberating the mass unconscious, expressing its innermost aspirations, telling it what it most wants to hear.'*

Extract taken from; Otto Strasser, *Hitler and I*, pages 74-77. Published by; Jonathan Cape Ltd., London, 1940.

Surely Strasser's words encapsulate the secret of Hitler's success through the years of struggle, then later, during the early years of his Chancellorship.

The ancient city of Nuremberg with its half-timbered buildings was heavily bombed by the RAF in early 1945. Even at that stage, Nuremberg was still a centre producing about half of Germany's aeroplane, submarine, and tank engines. On 2 January 1945, some 525 aircraft of the RAF destroyed approximately 90 per cent of the city. Why it was deemed necessary to flatten Nuremberg to that extent and, given that the Second World War was, by any stretch of the imagination virtually over at that point, is a matter for the conscience of those who took the decision. Nonetheless, Nuremberg has risen from the ashes. It is a vibrant city once more. Most of the destroyed buildings in the old town have been carefully restored and rebuilt.

Ironically, it was to Nuremberg, the city that had played host to the great Nazi rallies of the 1930s that the surviving Nazi leaders returned at the end of the Second World War. This time however, they were not there to celebrate, but to stand trial. Legal proceedings began on 20 November 1945 in Courtroom number 600 in the *Justizpalast* (Palace of Justice) located on Fürther Strasse. The trials would run for almost three and a half years, finally ending on 13 April 1949. Few of Hitler's former comrades would emerge from the proceedings with their lives. A number of the defendants, amongst them Hermann Göring, committed suicide during the trials; while others received the death sentence, the remainder received terms of life imprisonment.

'The victor will never be asked if he told the truth.' – Hitler

The following is a list of the twenty-one main defendants, those surviving Nazi leaders who stood trial at the *Justizpalast* in Nuremberg.

- Karl Doenitz; Admiral and Hitler's chosen successor. Served ten years in prison, released 1956.
- Hans Frank; Governor-General of occupied Poland. Hanged 16 October 1946.
- Wilhelm Frick; Reich Minister of the Interior. Hanged 16 October 1946.
- Hans Fritzsche; Head of the Radio Division in the Propaganda Ministry. Acquitted.
- Walther Funk; Minister of Economics. Life imprisonment, released in 1957 on health grounds.
- Hermann Göring; Chief of Luftwaffe and President of the Reichstag. Committed suicide 15 October 1946.
- Rudolf Hess; Deputy Führer and Nazi Party Leader. Life imprisonment, committed suicide 17 August 1987, aged 93.
- Alfred Jodl; Colonel General and Chief of Operations of German High Command. Hanged 16 October 1946.
- Ernst Kaltenbrunner; Head of *Reichssicherheitshauptamt* (RSHA) Reichs Central Security Office. Hanged 16 October 1946.
- Wilhelm Keitel; General Field Marshal and Chief of Staff of German High Command. Hanged 16 October 1946.
- Konstantin von Neurath; Minister for Foreign Affairs until 1938, then Reich Protector of Bohemia and Moravia. Sentenced to fifteen years, released in 1954 on health grounds.
- Franz von Papen; German Chancellor prior to Hitler, then Vice-Chancellor under Hitler. Acquitted.
- Erich Raeder; Admiral and Commander in Chief of German Navy.

- Life imprisonment, released in 1955 on health grounds.
- Joachim von Ribbentrop; Foreign Minister. Hanged 16 October 1946.
- Alfred Rosenberg; Nazi philosopher and Reich Minister for the Eastern Occupied Territories. Hanged 16 October 1946.
- Fritz Sauckel; Chief of Slave Labour Recruitment. Hanged 16 October 1946.
- Hjalmar Schacht; President of the Reichsbank. Acquitted.
- Baldur von Schirach; Reich Youth Leader.
  Sentenced to twenty years, released 1966.
- Artur Seyss-Inquart; Austrian Chancellor, then Reich Commissioner of occupied Netherlands. Hanged 16 October 1946.
- Albert Speer; Minister for Armaments and Munitions.
  Sentenced to twenty years, released 1966.
- Julius Streicher; Member of the Reichstag, ardent Anti-Semite and editor of *Der Stürmer* (The Stormer) an Anti-Jewish Magazine. Hanged 16 October 1946.

To conclude, it is probably fair to say that the political success of the Nazi Party was, to a great extent, based on the fact that the leadership had correctly identified, and then appeared to empathize with, the many deep-seated hopes and fears of the German people. The Nazis appeared to offer hope to a nation still trying to come to terms with the harshness of the much hated Versailles Treaty, high unemployment and economic collapse, particularly between 1929 and 1932. That said, Germany had made progress towards economic recovery through the late 1920s, and the country's acceptance into the League of Nations in 1926 went some considerable way to restoring her former international status. Even general public discontent was lessening. However, the aforementioned high unemployment combined with the terrible World Depression of 1930 played right into Hitler's hands. It was the coming together of these elements that created a situation that would lead to increased public support for the Nazis.

On coming to power in 1933 the Nazi Party successfully set about dealing with high unemployment and the ravages of a shattered economy. There were six million unemployed in Germany at the beginning of 1933. By 1939 that figure had been reduced to just over 300,000. It was in this way that the Nazis finally won acceptance and support across the social divides. Whilst through the early years of political struggle the Party had relied predominantly on the working class for its support, it could later count the middle and upper classes and members of the aristocracy amongst its supporters as hope and national pride were restored.

James Wilson
March 2011

Propaganda Postcards

The use of postcards for patriotic and propaganda reasons, in so far as Germany is concerned, dates from the early 1900s. The introduction of faster photographic techniques and production methods at that time permitted the distribution of postcards on a scale as never before. During the First World War, many firms (including the famous W. Sanke of Berlin) produced large numbers of posed studio images in postcard form depicting many of Germany's better known, high ranking military figures.

The arrival of the latest technological advances in military hardware, such as aircraft, U-boats and airships into that conflict contributed to the production of numerous postcards publicizing the new generation of young military hero. These were the men gaining fame and honour at what was then the 'cutting edge' of modern warfare. The availability of these postcards throughout Germany created an interest in collecting the sharp photographic images resulting from the latest processes.

Later, in 1933 when the Nazis came to power, the value of using postcards for propaganda purposes was fully realized and consequently used to maximum advantage and effect. The Propaganda Ministry of Dr Joseph Goebbels was highly efficient; it had determined that the postcard image could be personal, even intimate and strong in human interest. Here was a medium that could influence and inspire. With this in mind, the gargantuan machine that was the Propaganda Ministry went into overdrive, producing images of popular figures both political and military.

There followed a fantastic number of postcards showing the then rapidly expanding armed forces on manoeuvres with the latest equipment; so great was the interest that many military units were assigned their own photographer. These men were obliged to submit their work to the Propaganda Ministry where all images were selected and approved prior to production and release. If not selected for use as a postcard image the work of the unit photographer often found its way onto the pages of one or more of the many popular military magazines or newspapers of the day. Publications such as *'Der Adler'* (the air force magazine), *'Die Kriegsmarine'* (the naval magazine), *'Die Wehrmacht'* (combined armed forces magazine), *'Das Schwarze Korps'* (the SS magazine) or *'Signal'* (the largest selling wartime picture magazine in Europe, also under the control of Dr Goebbels) featured much of the work of these men.

Military, patriotic and politically motivated postcards were widely available throughout the Third Reich with outlets on virtually every street corner. The Nazi Party had a ready source of revenue through this medium, in addition to the almost unimaginable propaganda value it provided. Many such postcards were distributed in other countries through the various German embassies before the Second World War, thus many examples turn up bearing foreign stamps and postmarks.

On the political side it has to be said production was almost limitless, particularly where Hitler himself was concerned. Of all political and military figures of the twentieth century, Adolf Hitler probably remains the single, most photographed and filmed personality of all. Many such images (some the work of Hoffmann, Hitler's personal photographer) then reproduced in postcard form depict Hitler in incalculable situations

Reverse reads:
After an original painting by Hugo Lehmann.
Verlag Heinrich Hoffmann, München

This postcard is a reproduction of the original painting 'Der Führer' by artist Hugo Lehmann. Lehmann was one of the leading artists of the Third Reich, he died in 1941. He produced 'Der Führer' working from one of a series of photographs taken of Hitler on the evening that he announced the establishment of the Greater German Reich on 12 March 1938 in the Rathaus in Linz, Austria. As a young man, Hitler had lived in the village of Leonding just outside Linz. Hitler, an Austrian by birth, was made a German citizen on the evening of 12 March 1932 in Brunswick. Brunswick at the time was a Nazi-controlled state.

and locations, for example; speaking at rallies, meeting the people, with other heads of state, in his Berlin Reich's Chancellery, or relaxing at the Berghof, his alpine retreat on the Obersalzberg above Berchtesgaden. The variety is staggering. As with the majority of German postcards of the period these are high quality photographic prints and not, as one might imagine, machine printed examples, (these do exist, but on a lesser scale).

The idea that Germany's infrastructure had been completely destroyed in 1945 through Allied 'saturation bombing' is open to challenge; in so much that all the materials and equipment necessary for the production of postcards were still in place, right up until the last days of the war. Unit photographers were still in a position to acquire film, to have that film processed, to obtain photographic paper for printing and return the work to Berlin for approval.

In retrospect, this combined with the fact that the government departments responsible for the design and production of new postage stamps were still operating now seems inconceivable. This indicates that quantities of paper were available, electric power was in place and printing machinery functional. The idea that such things had been maintained at a time when priorities surely lay elsewhere, shows just how detached these bureaucrats were from the reality around them. That said, it also reveals how much emphasis had been placed on the postcard image, the believed effect it had in inspiring ordinary people and subsequently its contribution to maintaining a nation's morale.

The Nazis utilized this medium with great dexterity, to promote strength, a political idea and a way of life, using intensive and invasive propaganda techniques that were very much ahead of their time. Many of their methods of political campaigning and use of the media for electioneering purposes have been adopted by numerous post war politicians around the world. No other nation had come to recognize the potential or appeal of the postcard image for purely propaganda purposes during that period.

Nevertheless, it must be said that other countries did produce patriotic postcards; however they had little impact and were never produced on such a scale as in Hitler's Germany. We must conclude therefore, based on the evidence of the remaining postcards from the Nazi period that the quantity and variety of these images together with the demand for them, even by today's standards, was almost inexhaustible.

Author's Comment

At the risk of leaving myself open to criticism, I should point out that from the outset it has been my intention not to express any political opinions in this work. Furthermore, I have deliberately attempted neither to promote nor denounce any individual; rather it has been my intention to present the facts and to allow the reader to draw their own conclusions.

This intention might best be explained by way of the following scenario. Imagine you are a member of the working class living in 1920s Germany. While the defeat of 1918 still haunts the nation, the resulting shattered economy, uncontrolled rampant inflation and widespread unemployment are even harder to bear. The end of 1923 sees the beginning of sustained economic growth. This growth continues until halted by the catastrophic effects of the World Depression in 1930. Germany, perhaps more than any other country, is hardest hit.

Let us move forward, it is 1933 and the Nazis are in power, now try to imagine how you might react to a relentless, and as yet, never previously encountered sophisticated propaganda campaign. While there is no escaping the powerful symbolism of the new regime, there are frequent broadcasts applauding the achievements of the new political and social order. Where the unfortunate and, for the most part generally unpopular governments through the period of the Weimar Republic had failed; the Nazi Party's 'Four-Year Plan', introduced in 1933 to tackle unemployment and economic problems is now bearing fruit and changing people's lives.

It is now 1935 and the restrictions of the Versailles Treaty are being openly flouted, not least by the re-emergence of the military, and all it seems without any foreign reaction. Finally, there is a definite feeling of renewed national pride as the new government declares itself responsible for all the improvements in everyday life, with promises of better to come. Exciting times by any stretch of the imagination, don't you think! With that in mind, notwithstanding the terrible hidden agenda as yet to unfold, can we be sure, given the same set of circumstances that we would have reacted any differently. Who are we to judge?

Finally, and in order to better understand the captions that accompany the following images, it should be explained that all text shown in **'bold type'**, whether this appears as just part of the caption, or indeed the entire caption, is a translation of the original German text taken from that particular postcard. The reader should also understand that each caption has been composed to compliment and enhance the image to which it relates; this is a deliberate effort on my part in an attempt to replicate how these images would have been presented to the German public and the rest of the world at the time of their original release.

Images from the Early Days

1. Adolf Hitler.
This interesting postcard with the year 1928 written in pencil on the reverse reveals a somewhat younger Adolf Hitler. Then aged 39, the future Führer is observed wearing a pair of traditional lederhosen. His hair is combed back rather than down to the left side as was always the case in later years. Soon after he became Chancellor, Hitler banned the publishing of such photographs as he believed they portrayed him as rather too parochial.

2. *Reverse reads:* **National Party Day in Nuremberg 1929.**
This early postcard shows Adolf Hitler standing in an open-top motor car during the 1929 National Party Rally held in Nuremberg at the beginning of August that year. Standing on the running board of the vehicle is Franz Pfeffer von Salomon (1888–1968). Von Salomon was the first commander of the SA following the restoration of the Nazi Party on 27 February 1925. The SA had been disbanded following the failed Beer-Hall *Putsch* (Revolt) of 9 November 1923. Nonetheless, the organization continued to exist in an underground form through the period of the ban. The SA was re-established in November 1926. To the left of von Salomon stands his adjutant, Georg Hallermann. The scene has been photographed in front of the Frauenkirche in Nuremberg's Hauptmarkt.

Emil Kirdorf (1847-1938), a prominent Rhur industrialist was the guest of honour at the 1929 Party Rally. An early and loyal supporter of Adolf Hitler and the Nazi Party through the 1920s, the wealthy Kirdorf ran some of the largest coal mines in Europe. On the occasion of his 90th birthday on 10 April 1937, Kirdorf was presented with the Order of the German Eagle, Nazi Germany's highest decoration, by Adolf Hitler personally.

3. Uncaptioned.
This scene shows the Hauptmarkt crowded with members of the public, many with arms outstretched in salute. On the right of the image a military band plays as the columns of men march past. On the extreme left, and in shadow, Adolf Hitler can be seen standing in his vehicle while he observes the approaching columns make their way over the Fleischbrücke and towards the Hauptmarkt.

4. The Hauptmarkt photographed in 2010. Considering the damage that Nuremberg suffered during the Second World War as a direct result of Allied bombing, it is hardly surprising that few points of reference remain. One thing common to both images however, is the small balcony window seen beneath the wording 'Café Hauptmarkt' that appears on the wall of the building in the centre of previous postcard. Additionally, the small first floor terrace of the same building, seen crowded with people in the aforementioned postcard, also remains.

Reichsparteitag 1933

In July 1933 the city of *Nürnberg* (Nuremberg) was officially chosen as a permanent venue for all future *Reichsparteitage* (National Party Days). The fifth Nazi Party Rally, thereafter these rallies are generally referred to as the Nuremberg Rallies, was held in September that year, and subsequently every year until 1938. The 1933 Rally; *Der Parteitag des Sieges* (The Rally of Victory) was a five day event running from 30 August to 3 September. The Rally of Victory, as the title suggests, referred to the Nazi victory and Hitler's becoming German Chancellor on 30 January 1933. On Hitler's orders, Leni Riefenstahl, the Führer's favourite German film director, was persuaded to make the documentary film; *Der Sieg des Glaubens* (Victory of Faith) to record the event. *Der Sieg des Glaubens* premiered in Berlin on 1 December 1933.

The film would be a prequel to Riefenstahl's 1935 political documentary *Triumph des Willens* (Triumph of the Will). Much of the innovative camera work and clever editing observed in *Triumph des Willens* was already apparent in *Der Sieg des Glaubens*. The cast included Hitler, Hess, Göring, Streicher, Goebbels and Ernst Röhm, leader of the SA – *Sturmabteilung* (Storm Troopers). Initially well received, the film was withdrawn following an event referred to as 'The Night of the Long Knives', a purge carried out on 30 June 1934. Röhm, a long time supporter of Hitler, was suspected with others of planning a second revolution using the SA. Ernst Röhm and his co-conspirators were traced to Bad Wiessee. While many of those suspected of being involved died on the night, Röhm was executed two days later.

Thereafter there was to be no mention of Ernst Röhm, who, at the time of filming *Der Sieg des Glaubens* was the second most powerful figure in the Nazi Party. This decision was followed by an order that all copies of the film were to be destroyed. As a result only one or two copies of the film are known to exist.

The 1933 *Reichsparteitag* proved a great success. In addition to the programme of events staged at the rally grounds, the enthusiastic Party faithful observed and cheered the uniformed ranks of the various organizations as they marched through the flag decorated city on their way to the rally. At the same time, in the *Hauptmarkt* (Main Square) in the centre of the old town, Hitler and his entourage reviewed the passing columns from a specially constructed rostrum. The *Hauptmarkt* was renamed the Adolf-Hitler-Platz (Adolf Hitler Square) in 1933. The end result, as deliberately intended, was a strengthening of the bond between Hitler and the people.

Whilst those attending the great Nazi rallies of the 1930s observed the pulling power of the Party and its phenomenal organizational capabilities firsthand, regular radio broadcasts brought the message of the *Reichsparteitage* into almost every German living-room and across most of Europe. Essentially propaganda events, the Nuremberg Rallies played a vital role in promoting, and then hammering home the idea encompassed in a popular slogan of the time; *Ein Volk, ein Reich, ein Führer!* (One People, one Empire, one Leader!). As a result, those groups and individuals not in step with the new regime would find themselves more and more marginalized.

Hitler had wasted little time in using his powers as Chancellor. Through the summer of 1933 several decrees were issued. All political parties other than the NSDAP were abolished. The trade unions were suppressed, or if in special cases they were allowed to remain, it was only as branches of the Nazi Party. The majority of the trade unions were absorbed into the *Deutsche Arbeitsfront* (DAF; German Labour Front). The DAF, headed by Dr Robert Ley, was officially established on 10 May 1933. Furthermore, all Jews were to be excluded from the civil service. Broadcasting and the press were subject to control and censorship. Teaching in German schools and universities was to conform to Nazi doctrine and the Nazi *Weltanschauung* (World View), i.e. National Socialist philosophy and their view of the world.

5. *Reverse reads:* **Festival postcard. Reichsparteitag of the N.S.D.A.P. in Nürnberg 1-3 September 1933.**
A postcard designed to promote and advertise the first *Reichsparteitag* of the Nazi Party following Hitler's becoming Chancellor on 30 January 1933.

The theme of this rally; *Der Sieg des Glaubens* (Victory of Faith) celebrated Hitler's and the Nazi Party's success in achieving power earlier that year.

The rallies cleverly promoted Party ideals while presenting the Führer as an almost godlike figure, at the same time the Nazi Party began to take on the mantle of a religion.
This postcard was designed by Siegmund von Suchodolski (1875-1935).

6. *Reverse reads:* **Only Hitler's flags fly above all streets.**
This atmospheric image shows a part of Nuremberg Castle bedecked with Nazi flags. The ancient city, full of Germanic and imperial history stretches out below. The Nuremberg Rallies provided both the participants and the onlookers with a new sense of identity and self-confidence. Large military style parades had not been seen in Germany since the First World War. These rallies certainly struck a chord with the audience, reminding them of Germany's lost military strength. It was in this way that many were channelled towards National Socialism.

7. *Front reads:* **Fünferplatz with the tower of the Town Hall.**
Reverse reads: **Nürnberg – The city of the National Party Days.**
This postcard shows a part of the old town of Nuremberg adorned with flags and banners in preparation for the Annual Party Congress.

8. *Reverse reads:* **Nürnberg – The city of the National Party Days. Adolf-Hitler-Platz.**
Here we see the Hauptmarkt; from 1933 until 1945 known as the Adolf-Hitler-Platz. On the right stands the famous Nuremberg Fountain so often seen in many of the postcards and photographs depicting Hitler observing the many march-pasts during the *Reichsparteitage*. Behind the fountain we see the Rathaus. The large building on the left in the background with a high pitched roof is the St Sebalduskirche.

9. Reichsparteitag in Nürnberg. Solemn assembly in the Town Hall during the speech of the Reich Chancellor Adolf Hitler.
Hitler addresses members of the Party faithful in the Rathaus (Town Hall) in Nuremberg during the 1933 Party Rally. Standing on the stage in the background and, appearing particularly choir-like are members of the Hitler Youth together with a number of adults. Perhaps the evening began with the singing of nationalist songs and anthems prior to Hitler mounting the podium to deliver his speech.

10. Nürnberg, the city of the Reichsparteitag. Part of the Maxbrücke.
Yet another interesting view of the old city of Nuremberg. In the foreground and on the opposite bank of the river Pegnitz we see the Weinstadel and the water tower. Behind that we see the twin spires of the St Sebalduskirche. On the left and high in the background stands the Kaiserburg (Emperor's Castle).

11. Nürnberg – Adolf-Hitler-Platz with Beautiful Fountain.
Reproduced in postcard format this painting by Nuremberg artist Heinrich Karlicek shows the Schöner Brunnen (Beautiful Fountain) on the Adolf-Hitler-Platz. On the right stands the Rathaus (Town Hall). It was in this square that Hitler would review the seemingly never-ending march-pasts of the various Nazi organizations during the Party Rallies of the 1930s.

12. *Reverse reads:* **City of the National Party Rallies Nürnberg. Interior of the Luitpold Hall.**
This view of the interior of the Luitpold Hall shows the seating arrangements and the permanent decorations. Below the large Nazi banner at the opposite end of the hall we see the speaker's platform with Hitler's personal standard attached. The Führer would deliver many rousing speeches to the Party faithful in these surroundings. Constructed in 1906 for the Bavarian Jubilee Exhibition the Luitpold Hall could seat 16,000 people. Having acquired the building the Nazi Party then completely renovated the former machine hall and remodelled the façade in typical Third Reich style. The Luitpold Hall was badly damaged through Allied bombing raids during the Second World War, only the granite steps that led to the main entrance remain today.

13. Opening of the Party Congress.
This interesting postcard shows the members of the Nazi 'Old Guard' attending the opening of the 1933 Annual Party Congress in Nürnberg.

From left to right they are:

Dr Wilhelm Frick, Reich Minister of the Interior.
Dr Paul Joseph Goebbels, Reich Minister of Public Enlightenment and Propaganda.
Dr Hans Kerrl, Prussian Minister of Justice and Reich Minister without Portfolio.
Franz Xavier Schwarz, Treasurer of the NSDAP.
Viktor Lutze, Police President of Hanover, later Provincial Governor and State Councillor.
Adolf Hitler, Führer.
Rudolf Hess, Deputy Führer.
Julius Streicher, owner of *Der Stürmer* (The Stormer/The Attacker), an illustrated anti-Semitic newspaper and *Gauleiter* (District Leader) of Franconia.
Behind Hess stands SA-*Obergruppenführer* (Lieutenant General) Wilhelm Brückner, personal adjutant to Hitler until 1940.
Behind Streicher stands SS-*Obergruppenführer* (Lieutenant General) Julius Schaub, personal adjutant to Hitler after 1940.
Finally, and on the extreme right stands Martin Bormann, then Chief of Staff to Rudolf Hess.

14. *Reverse reads:* **Nürnberg Party Congress 1933. Congress Hall in the Luitpold Hall.**
The Congress Hall is filled to capacity. Enthusiastic Party members fill the hall as they await the Führer. Hitler often deliberately kept the crowd waiting in an attempt to build up the tension. He would then take to the podium to be greeted by an over-excited audience in an atmosphere often approaching hysteria.

15. Nürnberg Party Day 1933. The Führer and Chief of Staff Röhm during the honouring of the dead.
This superb, but rare postcard shows Adolf Hitler and Ernst Röhm, Head of the SA, standing together before the monument to the dead at a ceremony held during the Party Congress to honour the fallen comrades and those killed during the First World War. The monument, which still stands, then formed part of the Luitpold Arena, being located directly opposite the speaker's platform.

Hitler and Röhm would have marched the length of the paved *Straße des Führers* (the Führer's Way) connecting the two points to reach the monument. Captain Ernst Röhm was one of Hitler's earliest supporters; indeed it was Röhm who organised the SA along military lines. However, Röhm fell from grace in June 1934. Hitler, convinced that Röhm was planning a second revolution had his old friend arrested on 30 June 1934. Two days later Röhm was shot. Following this 'Blood Purge' also referred to as 'The Night of the Long Knives', all images of Röhm were removed from the Party's records.

16. *Reverse reads:* **The flags of the political organizations lower themselves before the martyrs of the movement. Party Congress 1933.**
With flags lowered SA troopers march past the monument to the dead in the Luitpold Arena during the 1933 Party Congress.

17. Uncaptioned.
This interesting early postcard shows Adolf Hitler and numerous leaders of the various Nazi organizations occupying the temporary wooden stands erected on the Zeppelin Field for the 1933 Party Congress. By 1934, work on the more permanent structures, those designed by Albert Speer, had begun on the Zeppelin Field.

18. *Reverse reads:* **The roll-call of the Political Officials. Entry of the flags during the Party Congress, Nuremberg 1933.**
Literally hundreds of Nazi flags are carried into the arena by men of the SA. The sight of hundreds and thousands of marching men, the uniforms, together with the many flags and banners carried during numerous parades and the torch-lit night-time processions could hardly fail to have an impact on the civilian observers. Each and every event during the Party Congress had been carefully orchestrated to make the observer feel that they were witnessing something extremely important and to invoke a sense of belonging.

19. *Reverse reads:* **National Party Day in Nürnberg 1933. The Führer consecrates the new assault flags.**

This fabulous image sees Hitler consecrating new flags during a ceremony at the 1933 Party Congress. The man carrying the *Blutfahne* (Blood Banner) is SS *Sturmbannführer* (Major) Jakob Grimminger. The *Blutfahne* was one of the most revered Party objects. It was carried during the Munich Beer-Hall *Putsch* (Revolt) in 1923 and had allegedly been stained by the blood of the Nazi martyrs who fell on the day. Hitler would consecrate new banners by touching them to the *Blutfahne*.

20. *Reverse reads:* **Nürnberg 1933. Marching up of the SA in the Luitpoldhain.**
Thousands of SA men gather on the Luitpoldhain during the 1933 Party Congress. The sight of seemingly endless columns of marching SA and SS men must have surely had an overwhelming effect upon the observing public attending the rallies. The whole event had been deliberately designed and orchestrated to give the impression of a reborn and powerful Germany under the direction of Hitler and the Nazi Party.

21. *Reverse reads:* **A hundred thousand men of the SA and SS at the Party Congress Nürnberg 1933.** In the foreground stand the men of the SS (*Schutzstaffel;* Elite Guard); in the background, beyond the first line of flags are men of the SA. The logistics required to successfully execute something on the scale of the Nuremberg Rallies must have been a great test for the organisers; and yet these huge events appear to have been carried off with typical German precision and efficiency.

Reichsparteitag 1934

The sixth Nuremberg Rally; *Der Parteitag der Einheit und Stärke* (The Rally of Unity and Strength) was a six day event that ran from 5 to 10 September 1934. This rally will always be remembered for the film *Triumph des Willens* (Triumph of the Will) by Leni Riefenstahl. The Führer had been at pains to persuade Riefenstahl to take on the job of directing the film; it was only with Hitler's personal guarantee that there would be no interference from any Party agencies that she finally agreed. Leni Riefenstahl would write, produce, direct and edit the film herself. The city of Nuremberg became a stage-set for Riefenstahl's epic. Despite the enormous budget the project presented Riefenstahl with numerous technical difficulties.

By introducing innovations such as aerial photography, moving cameras, telephoto lenses, together with the idea of combining music and film Riefenstahl set new standards in cinematography. The film premiered on 28 March 1935. The dramatic opening sequence shows a Junkers Ju52 aircraft passing through a cloudscape as it conveys the Führer to his people. Later, we see Rudolf Hess, Deputy Führer, thank those foreign visitors attending *Reichsparteitag* before introducing and praising Hitler in his opening address.

Hess, as every good PR man would, today we call them 'spin-doctors', works the audience. He whips the spectators into an emotional frenzy, looking directly at Hitler, Hess says; *'You are Germany! When you act, the nation acts; when you judge, the people judge'*. This statement is followed by rapturous applause from the entire audience with cries of *'Sieg Heil! Sieg Heil!'* (Hail to Victory!). Another sequence focuses on the Führer as he delivers a rousing address to the *Hitler Jugend* (HJ; Hitler Youth). In his address Hitler says; *'And I know that it cannot be otherwise – that you are the flesh of our flesh, and the blood of our blood; that in your young minds runs the same spirit that dominates us. You cannot be other than bound to us. And when the great columns march through the mists today, moving in triumph through Germany, I know that you will be marching side by side, and you know that Germany lies in front of us, Germany marches with us, and Germany marches behind us!'* Powerful words indeed; Hitler's oratory was probably his greatest weapon, and speeches such at these could hardly fail to impress young minds.

Triumph des Willens went on to win a number of awards for its director. Riefenstahl, who died in 2003 at the age of 101, could hardly have imagined the effect that *Triumph des Willens* would have on the world of film-making. Not least that her ground-breaking work in 1934 would continue to influence film-makers today. There is no escaping the emotional power of *Triumph des Willens*. Riefenstahl's skilled and imaginative filming has a way of stirring the emotions of her audience. On viewing the film today, one can see why the audiences of the 1930s came away with the feeling that they had witnessed something momentous, and how they were fortunate, indeed blessed to be living during this important period in their history.

Triumph of the Will is, without doubt, the most important surviving visual record of a period in recent history that shows not only the power of the Nazi movement, but how

22. *Reverse reads:* **Festival postcard. Party Congress of the N.S.D.A.P. in Nürnberg 5–10 September 1934.** One of a number of postcards designed to promote and advertise the second Party Congress of the Nazi Party in 1934. The theme of this rally; *Der Parteitag der Einheit und Stärke* (The Rally of Unity and Strength). This postcard was designed by Prof. Richard Klein (1890-1967).

the persona of Adolf Hitler was cultivated and projected to a point where ordinary people came to see Hitler as their saviour. Whilst initially a political movement, the NSDAP later sought to influence the very thinking of an entire nation with the determination of a religious zealot as the idea of the Hitler cult became ever more evident.

As Hitler said, *'Those who see in National Socialism nothing more than a political movement know scarcely anything of it. It is more even than religion; it is the will to create mankind anew.'*

On 5 September 1934 the Führer appeared in the Congress Hall adjacent to the Luitpold Arena. The band played 'The Badenweiler March' as Hitler, followed by Göring, Goebbels, Hess, Himmler, and several aides made their way to the large stage. When they were seated, and following an address by Rudolf Hess, Adolf Wagner, *Gauleiter* (District Leader) of Bavaria read the following Führer proclamation. *'The German form of life is definitely determined for the next thousand years. The Age of Nerves of the nineteenth century has found its close with us. There will be no other revolution in Germany for the next one thousand years!'*

Such was the confidence with which Hitler sat upon the stage before an audience of 30,000 people. The German Army was already bound in obedience to Hitler through the oath that all members had sworn the year previously. During these early years Adolf Hitler would prove a dynamic, mesmerising, almost irresistible force to a nation now beginning to reap the benefits of economic revival and re-emerging national pride. Through the mid 1930s Hitler enjoyed a popularity the like of which most politicians can only dream of.

On the evening of 7 September 1934 Hitler addressed some 200,000 party faithful gathered on the Zeppelin Field. Raised amidst the ranks of these perfect formations on the field were over 20,000 unfurled Nazi flags. This, together with Albert Speer's inspired and imaginative lighting effects where some 130 anti-aircraft searchlights set at 12 metre (40 feet) intervals cast beams of light directly up into the night sky to a height of over 7,500 metres (25,000 feet) completely mesmerised the onlookers. Climbing high into a clear night sky these beams converged at their apex to form a dome. Speer's, as he described it, 'Cathedral of Light' effect, has been described by others as a 'Cathedral of Ice'.

On 10 September, designated Army Day, motorized army units using the most modern equipment carried out manoeuvres on the Zeppelin Field. This was the first time since the First World War that the German public had seen a large military display. For those attending the rally one the highlights was a fake, yet remarkably realistic battle. The 300,000 audience were suitably impressed and became very excited. When Hitler finished speaking at the end of the military display, the crowd cheered for so long that when Hess got up to speak it was some time before he could be heard.

The running order of the programme for the 1934 Nazi Party Congress was as follows:

Tuesday 4 September: **Day of Greeting.**
Reception for the international press in the Germanic Museum.
Speaker: Ernst Hanfstaengl.
Press reception in the *Kulturvereinshaus*. Speaker: Dr Otto Dietrich.
Reception for Hitler's arrival at the *Rathaus* (City Hall).
Speakers: *Oberbürgermeister* (Lord Mayor) Willy Liebel and Adolf Hitler.

Wednesday 5 September: **Day of the Opening of the Nazi Party Congress.**
Congress meeting in the Luitpold Hall. Speakers: Rudolf Hess and Julius Streicher.
Reading of Hitler's proclamation for the Nazi Party Congress.
Meeting on cultural matters in the Apollo Theatre.
Speakers: Alfred Rosenberg and Adolf Hitler.

Thursday 6 September: **Day of the RAD; Reich Labour Service.**
Review of the Reich Labour Service on the Zeppelin Field.
Speakers: Konstantin Hierl and Adolf Hitler.
Congress meeting in the Luitpold Hall.
Speakers: Joseph Goebbels, Robert Ley and Adolf Wagner.

Friday 7 September: **Day of the Political Organizations.**
Review of the Political Organizations on the Zeppelin Field. Speakers: Robert Ley and Adolf Hitler.
Congress meeting in the Luitpold Hall. Speaker: Walter Darré.
Meeting of the NSKOV – National Socialist War Victims' Care Organization in the *Kulturvereinshaus.* Speaker: Hanns Oberlindober.

Saturday 8 September: **Day of the Hitler Youth.**
Review of the Hitler Youth in the Luitpold Arena.
Speakers: Baldur von Schirach and Adolf Hitler.
Meeting of the Nazi Women's Association in the Luitpold Hall. Speaker: Adolf Hitler.
Meeting of the Reich's Labour Service leaders in the *Kulturvereinshaus.*
Speaker: Konstantin Hierl.

23. *Reverse reads:* **City of the Party Congress Nürnberg. Bird's-eye view of the model of the Party Rally Grounds.**
This early architectural model shows the intended layout of the Rally Grounds. The bulk of what we see here was planned by Albert Speer. Much of the planned construction seen in the model would never be completed. The rectangular area observed upper left on the model is the Märzfeld. This was to be a parade ground and exercise area for the Wehrmacht. Work on the Märzfeld did not begin until 1938 and at the end of the war only eleven of the planned twenty-four gate-towers had been built. Nothing of the Märzfeld remains. At the opposite end of the 'Great Road', seen running diagonally from the Märzfeld and through the centre of the image, we see the planned 'D' shaped Congress Hall. The Congress Hall, while only partly completed, is the largest single structure from the Nazi period to remain standing. Opposite this new Congress Hall, and work on the building did not begin until 1935, stands the old Congress Hall, formerly the Luitpold Hall, and below that the Luitpold Arena.

Sunday 9 September: **Day of the SA and SS.**
Review of the SA and the SS in the Luitpold Arena. Speakers: Viktor Lutze and Adolf Hitler.

Monday 10 September: **Day of the Army.**
Congress meeting in the Luitpold Hall. Speaker: Adolf Hitler.
Closing ceremony of the Nazi Party Congress.

24. Uncaptioned.
This wonderful image shows a column of SA men marching through the old part of the city. The Führer, arm outstretched in salute, stands in his open-top Mercedes as the column reaches the Adolf-Hitler-Platz. The temporary grandstand on the right is filled with enthusiastic people who are also seen to salute those marching past. The 'Gothic spire' type structure in the background behind Hitler's car is the famous Nuremberg Fountain; behind the fountain stands the Rathaus (Town Hall).

25. Uncaptioned.
Text next to image reads: **Festival postcard for Reichsparteitag, Price 25 Rpf. including cultural donation.**

While the image on this postcard is almost identical to that of postcard number 30, this is a good example of the type of commemorative and politically motivated postcard that was on sale to the general public during the annual Party Congress. While at first glance one might be inclined to dismiss the humble postcard and its role in spreading a political message, we should, perhaps, look at it a little more closely.

The postcard was an important tool in the Nazi propaganda arsenal. The images chosen for postcard purposes were not chosen randomly, but carefully selected for both their content and their perceived impact on the general public. In buying a postcard such as the above, the purchaser was promoting Nuremberg, the spiritual centre of the Party, the Party Rallies, the Nazi Party, and Adolf Hitler. Additionally, the purchaser was also making a 'cultural donation' as stated on the postcard itself.

26. Nürnberg. The city of the Reichsparteitage. Monument in the Luitpold Arena.
The large structure in the background is the war memorial to Germany's war dead, those who fell during the First World War, erected in 1929. In the foreground stands the *Führerempore* (Führer's rostrum) from where Hitler would deliver many stirring speeches. A paved walkway of granite slabs, the *Straße des Führers* (the Führer's Way) connected the rostrum and the monument in the background. When completed, the Luitpold Arena could accommodate up to 150,000 people. It was here that the mass assemblies and parades of the SA and the SS took place before the Führer, and here that the Nazi's held their most solemn rituals in remembrance of both the war dead and the Nazi martyrs of the failed 1923 Beer-Hall *Putsch* (Revolt). Today only the original monument constructed in 1929 remains standing.

27. Nürnberg. Tribune with the Führer's Way in the Luitpold Arena.
Looking back down the granite slab paved walkway observed in the previous postcard number 26 towards the Führer's rostrum located before the doorway beneath the central banner. Two enormous bronze eagles adorn the columns at either end of the structure. The lone soldier on guard close to the war memorial looks towards the photographer.

28. Nürnberg. National Eagle in the Luitpold Arena.
A close-up of one of the two magnificent Kurt Schmid-Ehmen designed bronze eagles that dominated either end of the Tribune in the Luitpold Arena. Working mainly in bronze and stone, Kurt Schmid-Ehmen (1901-1968) was a sculptor of world renown. His work through the Nazi period was used to adorn numerous structures. Interestingly, this postcard was posted by a soldier serving in a Flak company based in Fürth, northeast of Nuremberg on 21 June 1943 to an address in Spandau, Berlin.

29. The Führer proceeds to the honouring of the heroes with the roll-call of the SA, SS and the NSKK.
Having left the speaker's rostrum seen on the right, Hitler, flanked by Heinrich Himmler (right), and, following the removal of Ernst Röhm, the new head of the SA, Viktor Lutze (left), makes his way down the steps that lead to the Führer's Way as all three make their way towards the monument located at the other end of the walkway.

30. Honouring the dead.
Reverse reads: **Party Congress 1934. Memorial.**

Hitler (centre), flanked by Heinrich Himmler (left) and Viktor Lutze (right), having walked the length of the granite paved *Straße des Führers* in total silence give the Nazi salute before the Ehrenhalle (War Memorial) to the fallen comrades; and to the *Blutfahne* (Blood Banner) carried by SS *Sturmbannführer* (Major) Jakob Grimminger (centre). The *Straße des Führers* was 240 metres long and 18 metres wide.

The massed uniformed ranks of 150,000 SA and SS men in the background stand silently at attention in solemn remembrance. This photograph has been taken from a point inside the Ehrenhalle located behind the flag bearer. Posted to an address in Munich on 8 September 1934; the sender then indicates his place amongst the massed ranks, both in the message on the reverse, and again on the photograph itself by placing an 'x' on the right hand side of the image.

31. *Reverse reads:* **The roll-call of the SA, SS and NSKK at the Party Congress in Nürnberg. General view of the Luitpold Arena lined with the formations during the roll-call. The Führer speaks.**
Without doubt the Nuremberg Rallies remain the most powerful and carefully orchestrated mass propaganda events ever staged. This absolutely fabulous folding postcard image surely translates that statement into visual form. To the left of the fold in the centre of the image, and about two thirds across from the three huge hanging banners, we see the figure of Adolf Hitler standing on the speaker's rostrum. On the right of the image, and at the opposite end of the *Straße des Führers* (the Führer's Way) stands the memorial already discussed in caption 26. The massed ranks of the SA, the SS and the NSKK, 150,000 men, stand silently at attention in the arena. The public stands in the far distance on the right are filled to bursting as all present listen attentively while Hitler delivers his address.

It is small wonder that those in attendance were overwhelmed and intoxicated by the scale and precision with which these huge events were carried out. Again, it is hardly surprising that these and other suchlike events had their effect upon Hitler himself. The idea of the Führer 'cult' was born out of a nation's desperate desire to find a leader who promised a way out of the economic disaster that had engulfed Germany between the wars. Hitler, it seemed, offered the right solutions. The prosperity that the Nazi regime brought about during the mid 1930s served to cement Hitler's relationship with the German people, but more importantly, these events and the adoration of the masses served to fuel Hitler's belief in his own infallibility.

32. Uncaptioned. *(right)*
Members of the SA vie for a space in the Luitpold Arena at the conclusion of the day's official proceedings. While some of the men stand around chatting, others are seen sitting, however a few of those photographed have managed to find enough space to lie stretched out on the ground.

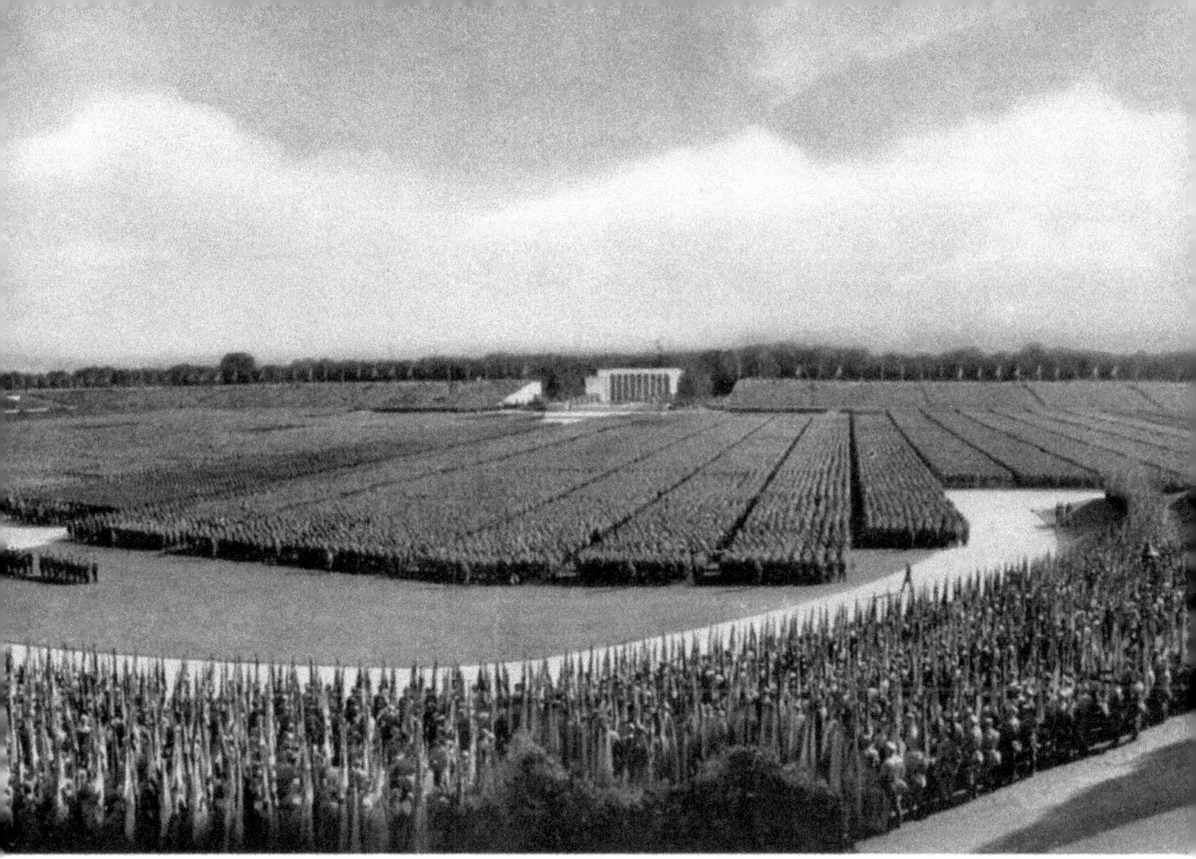

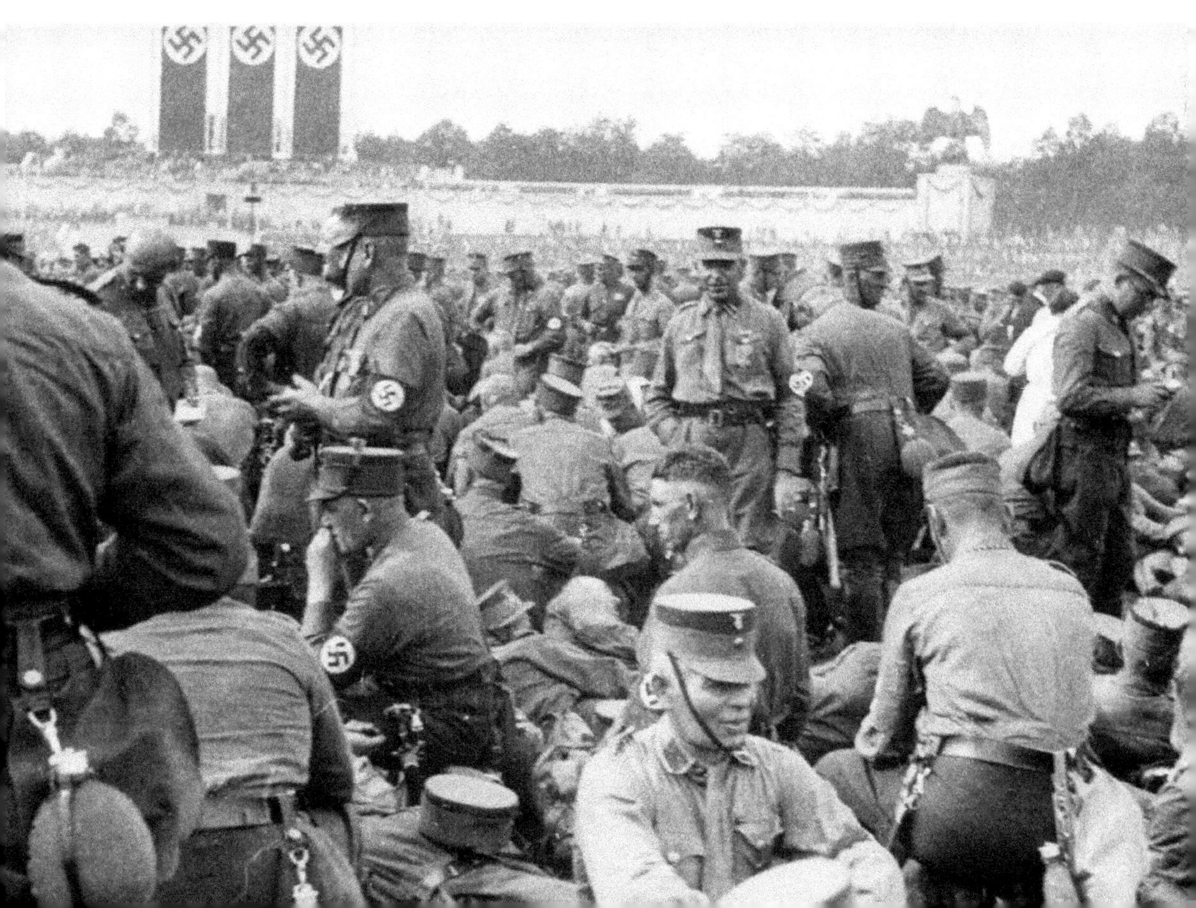

33. Nürnberg 'Luitpold Arena with Congress Hall.'
This aerial view of the Luitpold Arena and Congress Hall shows members of the public walking around the site. The scale of the structures and the many banners combine to create a powerful impression - as was their aim. Before the three large Nazi banners on the right and at the end of the central paved *Straße des Führers* stands the speaker's platform. Standing on this platform Adolf Hitler addressed the gathered multitudes.

34. Nürnberg Congress Hall in the Luitpold Arena.
The main entrance to the Congress Hall (also referred to as the Luitpold Hall). This image shows the main entrance to the building following the Nazi reconstruction of the frontage of the former machine hall built in 1906. While numerous Nazi banners hang on the front of the building, it is the Führer's personal standard that dominates, taking pride of place above the main portal. In the foreground we see some of the newly-constructed grandstands.

52

*Reichsparteitag Nürnberg
Der Führer begrüsst
Reichswehrminister von Blomberg*

35. National Party Day Nürnberg.
The Führer greets Reichswehrminister (Minister of Defence) von Blomberg.
Adolf Hitler shakes hands with *Generaloberst* (Colonel-General; after April 1936 General Field Marshal) Werner von Blomberg during the 1934 *Reichsparteitag*. Those in uniform in the foreground and those members of public in the background raise their arms in salute to the two men. Von Blomberg (1878-1946) had served with distinction during the First World War, winning the Pour le Mérite. Hitler appointed him Minister of Defence in 1933. It was von Blomberg's idea to have all German soldiers swear a personal oath of allegiance to Adolf Hitler.

Of the following eight photographs, images numbers 36, 37, 38, 39, 40 and 42 are contemporary photographs taken by an unknown individual attending the 1934 Nuremberg Rally. These photographs show a number of well-known buildings, some of which still stand. Photographs numbers 41 and 43 were taken in 2010. These two photographs enable the reader to draw comparisons and see the dramatic changes that have taken place through the intervening years.

36. Uncaptioned.
The Königstr. with a view of the Lorenzkirche in the background. The building on the right, with the distinctive RAD flag hanging from the second-floor balcony is the Hotel Kaiserhof at 39 Königstr. Flags and banners of all sizes hang from the buildings along both sides of the street. It has been said that Hitler, during the early years, expressed a wish to stay at the Kaiserhof during his visits to Nuremberg. However, his request was declined. Hitler then chose the Hotel Deutscher Hof where he was made welcome. Later, as his popularity grew and it appeared likely that he might be elected Chancellor, Hitler received an invitation from the Kaiserhof to stay there. This was the hotel that had politely refused his earlier request. Hitler sent a reply stating that the Deutscher Hof met all his requirements and that he was happy to remain there.

37. Uncaptioned.
Another view of the Königstr. again with the Hotel Kaiserhof on the right. The streets are packed with men in uniform and members of the public. Nuremberg was a city filled to bursting during Party Congress as hundreds of thousands travelled from all over the Reich to attend one of the most important events in the Nazi calendar.

38. Uncaptioned.
Nuremberg's Pfannenschmiedsgasse, the buildings almost completely hidden behind a sea of huge Nazi banners are the Hotel Wittelsbacher Hof and the Apollo Theatre located at 22 Pfannenschmiedsgasse. Hitler addressed smaller groups at meetings held in the Apollo Theatre during *Reichsparteitag*. The sun is shining on this fine September day and all attending the parades and Party Congress are guaranteed a memorable time.

39. Uncaptioned.
Flag-bearing men in uniform gather in front of the Hotel Wittelsbacher Hof. Members of the public collect on the corner. They may be commenting on the scene unfolding before them or perhaps planning their day's itinerary, while others appear more interested in photographing the flag-bearers.

40. Uncaptioned.
Yet another view of the Hotel Kaiserhof with that distinctive RAD flag hanging from the balcony. However, more interesting perhaps is the site of a well-known high-street name in this photograph, that of F. W. Woolworth.

41. The same scene photographed in 2010. It is quite amazing to think that F. W. Woolworth have occupied the same building for the best part of eighty years. Particularly when one considers the amount of near total devastation caused to Nuremberg's buildings through almost continuous air-raids during the latter stages of the Second World War.

42. Uncaptioned.
Nuremberg's Königstr. looking back towards the Königstorturm (King's Gate Tower), a part of the old city walls. In the background on the right, outside the ancient city walls, we see part of the Hauptbahnhof (Main Train Station). The whole city is geared up for the 1934 Party Congress, flags and banners hang from every building.

43. The same scene photographed in 2010. In comparing this photograph with the previous image number 42, we can see that apart from the Königstorturm, common to both photographs, there is hardly anything to indicate that we are observing the same scene. With the exception of the Königstorturm, there is no longer anything to connect these two images in any real sense.

44. German Combat Games 1934 - Nürnberg.
Groups from the various Nazi organizations gather in the Luitpold Arena for what the caption describes as 'Combat Games' during the 1934 Party Rally. The musicians of the army band in the centre stand silently at attention before those gathered on the field as all present await their instructions. This postcard-sized image may well be a privately taken photograph. The scene draws one to the conclusion that those assembled may be awaiting the Führer's arrival prior to beginning the exercises.

45. *Reverse reads:* **Party Congress Nürnberg 1934. Roll-call of the Political Leaders on the Zeppelin Field.**

One of the many evening/night-time gatherings that were held on the Zeppelin Field. Below the large eagle in the background stands the speaker's rostrum with a large Nazi banner attached. These night-time displays, featuring thousands of flag-bearing SA men and torchlight processions certainly captured the imagination of the onlookers. These powerful displays, full of ritual and harking back to ancient times, certainly provoked strong emotions amongst those present. The Zeppelin Field had an interior area of 312 x 285 metres, more than twelve football pitches. The field could accommodate up to 250,000 participants. Of all the planned construction work for the Rally Grounds, the Zeppelin Field with its Tribune was the only structure ever to be fully completed.

Reichsparteitag 1935

The seventh Nuremberg Rally; *Der Parteitag der Freiheit* (The Rally of Freedom) ran from 10 to 16 September 1935. In many ways this particular rally was a double celebration. The event not only celebrated, but openly drew attention to the recent re-introduction of compulsory military service in Germany, additionally, and perhaps more importantly, this meant that Germany was finally shaking off the constraints of the much hated Versailles Treaty. The First World War ended on 11 November 1918. The Versailles Treaty, referred to by the Germans as the *Versailles Diktat* (Versailles Dictation) because to them it seemed as if the harsh terms of the treaty had been deliberately designed to destroy Germany was signed on 28 June 1919.

Sections of the treaty placed specific restrictions on Germany's military capability; these included the size of the army, and the development of aircraft for military purposes. In March 1935, just six months prior to that year's *Reichsparteitag,* Hitler had announced the existence of the new German *Luftwaffe* (Air Force) to the world. While the very existence of this new German Air Force clearly defied the conditions of the Versailles Treaty, the reaction on the part of the western Allies at the time was that of collective indifference.

The Führer had declared himself a man of peace; Britain, and while perhaps to a lesser extent, France, took him at his word. Hitler stated that he was merely restoring self-respect to the German people, by giving them the right, as possessed by other nations, to defend themselves. The British agreed, and stated that they themselves would have done exactly the same under similar circumstances. The lack of any serious Allied response to Hitler's announcement on the *Luftwaffe* in March 1935, or to the fact that conscription had also been introduced in March that year, meant that the Nazis viewed their position as virtually unassailable; and that they could make any further announcements at that year's *Reichsparteitag* with impunity.

Another success in 1935 had been the peaceful return of the Saar, a region bordering France, Luxembourg and the German Rhineland. The Saarland had been German territory until the end of the First World War. Highly industrialized and rich in coal, the Saarland, with a population of over 800,000 had been under French administration since 1920. A plebiscite held on 13 January 1935 saw over 90 per cent of the population vote in favour of joining the German Reich. A meeting of the League of Nations Council approved the move four days later on 17 January. On 1 March 1935 the area was returned to Germany. The Führer was delighted. Nazi propaganda made much of the return of the Saarland. This was Hitler's first move in his plans to free Germany of the constraints of the Versailles Treaty and a diplomatic success to be paraded at the Party Congress later that year. The acquisition of the Saarland was the first territorial expansion of the Third Reich.

This was the first time that units of the new German Army had taken part in the parades. On 16 September, the last day of the rally, Hitler addressed the army formations assembled on the Zeppelin Field. Speaking on the subject of German military tradition he said; *'In war the nation's greatest defence, in peace the splendid school of our people.*

46. German Unity – German Power!
Reverse reads: **Festival postcard. Party Congress of the N.S.D.A.P. in Nürnberg 10–16 September 1935.**
Flag-bearing SA men stand shoulder to shoulder before the Nazi eagle. This particularly powerful image was just one of a number to appear as postcards designed to promote and advertise the seventh Party Congress of the Nazi Party in 1935.

The theme of this rally; *Der Parteitag der Freiheit* (The Rally of Freedom) celebrated the re-introduction of conscription, an act in open defiance of the much hated Versailles Treaty. This postcard was designed by Hans Schweitzer (1901-80). Schweitzer signed his work 'Mjölnir'.

It is the Army which has made men of us all, and when we looked upon the Army our faith in the future of our people was always reinforced. This glorious old Army is not dead; it only slept, and now it has arisen again in you.'

The short documentary film; *Tag der Freiheit: Unsere Wehrmacht* (Day of Freedom: Our Armed Forces) was Leni Riefenstahl's third film covering the Nuremberg Rallies. The film was made in response to a number of vocal protests by several army generals who had complained about the minimal army presence in *Triumph des Willens* the previous year. Directed, produced and written by Riefenstahl, *Tag der Freiheit: Unsere Wehrmacht* was released on 30 December 1935. A high point in the film was a mock battle staged by members of the Wehrmacht and the first public appearance of Germany's new *Panzerkampfwagen I* (Armoured Combat Car I) tank. Again the development of tanks by Germany was forbidden under the terms of the Versailles Treaty. Yet again the Allied response was limited, confined to nothing more than a number of paper protests. For many years it was believed that no copies of *Tag der Freiheit* had survived the Second

World War. However an incomplete copy with a running time of just twenty-eight minutes was found in the 1970s.

For all its usual pageantry, the 1935 *Reichsparteitag* remains significant for more sinister reasons, in that it was during this Rally that the Nazi Party announced the introduction of the 'Nuremberg Laws on Citizenship and Race,' these are generally referred to as the *Nürnberger Gesetze* (Nuremberg Laws). Hitler summoned the Reichstag to Nuremberg for a special sitting in order to have these new laws drawn up and passed. It was also during this 'special sitting' of the Reichstag that the swastika flag was declared Germany's new national flag. On 15 September these new laws were proclaimed to the Party Congress. The *Nürnberger Gesetze* actually became law on 30 September 1935.

The first of these; **The Law for the Protection of German Blood and German Honour**, forbids marriages, more than that, it specifically forbids extramarital sexual intercourse between 'Jews' and 'Germans', now clearly defined as being two separate races. Here, the word 'German' was followed by the term 'kindred blood', meaning anyone of Aryan blood. Additionally, 'German' females under the age of forty-five could not be employed by 'Jews' as domestic workers.

47. *Reverse reads:*
Festival postcard. Reichsparteitag of the N.S.D.A.P. in Nürnberg 10–16 September 1935.
This was the first in the series of the so called 'Red Cards' introduced to promote and advertise the 1935 Party Congress. Yet again, dramatic imagery is used to captivate and inspire the observer.

This postcard was designed by Prof. Richard Klein. The card was posted in Nuremberg on 14 September 1935 by someone attending the *Reichsparteitag*. It carries greetings to friends back in Munich.

The second law; **The Reich Citizenship Law**, took away the right of German citizenship from anyone considered not to be of German blood. Whether or not a person was of German blood was decided by using the following formula. A person with four German grandparents was considered to be of German blood. A person was classified as a Jew if they were descended from three or more Jewish grandparents. While a person descended from one or two Jewish grandparents was classified a *Mischling* (half-breed) of 'mixed blood'. In reality, the Nuremberg Laws simply legalized those measures already in place prior to their introduction. Furthermore, 'Jews' were denied the right to display the Reich or national flag; however, they were permitted to display the Jewish colours.

The introduction of the Nuremberg Laws brought about economic sanctions against Germany. In reality these sanctions had little effect other than to harden Nazi attitudes towards the Jews. Those with the foresight to see what was coming and the means to escape left Germany. That said, many countries that would now claim to have been instrumental in voicing their disapproval of Nazi Germany's treatment of the Jews in the 1930s refused to accept Jewish refugees at the time, or placed strict limitations on the numbers they would accept.

48. Nürnberg. Reichsparteitag Rally Grounds in the Luitpold Arena.
This postcard is obviously a composite, made up of three different elements found around the Luitpold Arena. On the left we see the Congress Hall. In the centre it is one of the two huge eagles that stood on columns located at either end of the Tribune that dominates the image. Finally, on the right we see the *Führerempore* (Führer's rostrum) with the three huge banners behind it.

49. *Reverse reads*: **Preparations for the 1935 Party Congress. The Führer discusses the review.**
An apparently rather excited Hitler discusses the march-past and review with SA leaders. On the right in SS uniform is Hitler's adjutant, Julius Schaub. Schaub had served with the German Army during the First World War. He had been involved in the 1923 *Putsch* (Revolt) and had subsequently served time in prison. Julius Schaub became Hitler's adjutant in 1925 and was thereafter constantly at the Führer's side. His rank, after 1944, was that of SS *Obergruppenführer* (Lieutenant-General). Schaub died in 1967.

50. March-past of the SA, SS and NSKK before the Führer. Reichsparteitag 1935.
Members of the various Nazi organizations parade before their Führer in the Adolf-Hitler-Platz during the 1935 Nuremberg Rally. Standing in his Mercedes, Hitler salutes the marching men. In the background we see the Gothic spire that is the Nuremberg Fountain. The large building in the background is the Rathaus. The NSKK; *Nationalsozialistisches Kraftfahrerkorps* (National Socialist Motor Corps) was a special motorized unit overseeing the preliminary training of recruits going on to serve in motorized and armoured units in the German Army.

51. Reverse reads: **The Rally of Freedom. The Führer awaits the brown columns.**
This superb image sees a composed Hitler awaiting the march-past of the SA, the Brownshirts. The Führer wears his *Eisernes Kreuz* (Iron Cross First Class) that he won during the First World War, in 1918. While rarely awarded to officers, it was almost unheard of that the Iron Cross should be awarded to someone serving in the non-commissioned ranks, and yet, Adolf Hitler had earned this much coveted award. Below the Iron Cross he wears the Black Wound Award (issued in black for one or two wounds) that he received in 1916 when he was wounded in the leg on the Somme. To the left stands Viktor Lutze, head of the SA. Behind Lutze stands Rudolf Hess, Deputy Führer. In the background on the left we see the St Sebalduskirche and on the right the Rathaus.

52. *Reverse reads:* **Motorized SA before the Führer at the 1935 Reichsparteitag.**
The Führer salutes motorized units of the SA entering the Adolf-Hitler-Platz at the 1935 *Reichsparteitag*. The columns of marching men stretch back to the Fleischbrücke. Hermann Göring (1893-1946) stands directly below Hitler's outstretched arm. On 1 March 1935 Göring had been named *Oberbefehlshaber der Luftwaffe* (Commander in Chief of the Air Force).

53. The Führer at the march-past. Reichsparteitag 1935.
Hitler, together with a number of leaders of the various Nazi organizations salutes the flag-bearers of the SA at the march-past in the Adolf-Hitler-Platz in the heart of the old city of Nuremberg. The temporary wooden terraces in the background are filled to capacity with members of the public who have travelled from every corner of the Reich to attend the event.

54. The coming together of the flags of the old army through the armed services.
Members of all branches of the Wehrmacht (the collective name for the combined armed services after 21 May 1935) carry the flags of the old Imperial Army through the streets of Nuremberg during the 1935 Party Rally. This calculated and emotive act would help strengthen and support the notion of a strong link between the much revered old Imperial Army and the new Wehrmacht. Hitler was fully aware of the significance and importance of such things.

55. *Reverse reads:* **Reichsparteitag in Nürnberg 1935: The flags of the glorious old army on the Day of the Wehrmacht.**
Enthusiastic crowds salute the standards of the old Imperial Army as they are carried through the city during the 1935 Party Congress. Hitler knew the importance of tradition, particularly when it came to the army. He knew well that the Prussian officer class would frown upon him and the Nazi regime. For that reason Hitler upheld and steadfastly supported the military traditions of the German Army; while it suited him, and pacified the officer corps.

56. *Reverse reads:* **Speaker's Rostrum in the Luitpold Arena at the Party Rally Grounds in Nürnberg.**

An excellent close-up of the *Führerempore* (Führer's rostrum) in the Luitpold Arena. Standing on the rostrum Hitler could look down on as many as 150,000 gathered in the arena. His speeches were specifically tailored to stir the emotions of those who, standing silently before him, listened attentively to every word. Individuals who attended such events in the 1930s have stated that, regardless of the size of the audience, everyone there felt that Hitler was, in some inexplicable way, speaking to them personally. Directly below the rostrum we see the beginning of the *Straße des Führers* (the Führer's Way) that led to the Ehrenhalle (War Memorial) opposite.

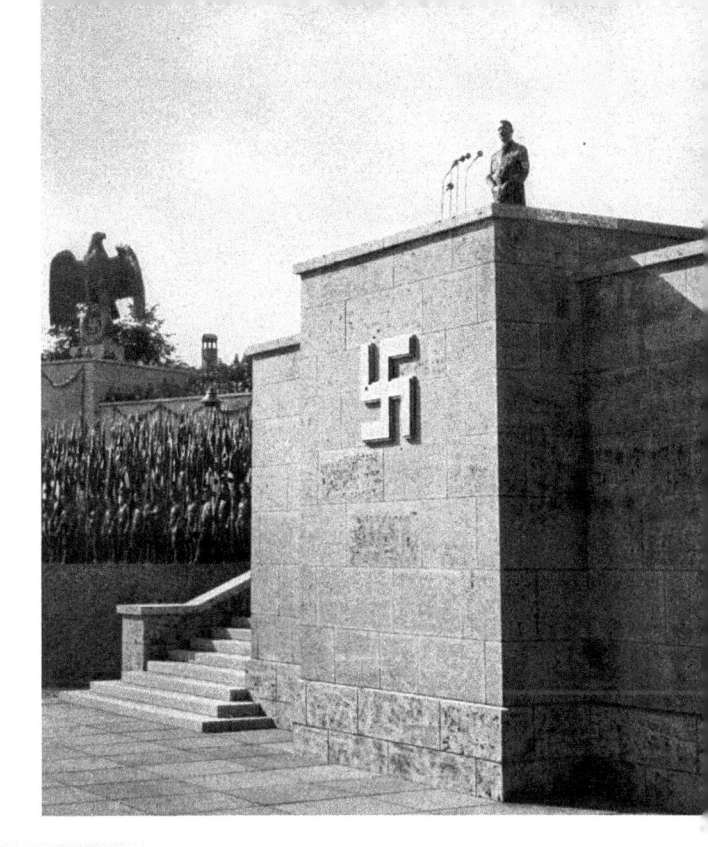

57. Uncaptioned.

This striking image, bearing no photographer or publisher details, shows a group of flag-bearing SA men standing before one of the two enormous bronze eagles found at either end of the Tribune in the Luitpold Arena. The scale of these symbols of Nazi power, designed and sculpted by Kurt Schmid-Ehmen is better understood if, when looking at the eagle, we compare it to the size of the men standing on top of the column directly beneath it.

Standing 7 metres tall, these magnificent bronze eagles had a wingspan of 7.5 metres; each weighed around 7.500 kilos.

71

58. *Reverse reads:* **Party Congress 1935. Dedicating the banners and honouring the dead.**
In a scene reminiscent of a Caesar addressing the legions of ancient Rome, Hitler, flanked by Himmler (left), and Lutze (right), addresses the assembled multitudes of SA and SS men in the Luitpold Arena. In the foreground the men of the SA carry the Nazi banners so often seen in surviving film footage of the many processions during the Nuremberg Rallies. In the background behind the massed ranks of the SS stands the Ehrenhalle. The ritual and ceremony connected with these enormous events and the way they were played out and then presented to the general public through postcards, newspapers, radio reports, then later television, could hardly fail to impress.

59. *Reverse reads:* **Hitler with the youth at the 1935 Party Congress.**
Hitler, standing in his open-top Mercedes salutes the members of the *Hitler Jugend* (Hitler Youth) as he is driven around the Luitpold Arena. Also in the photograph are, left to right; Deputy Führer, Rudolf Hess; Hitler's SS adjutant, Julius Schaub; and Hitler Youth Leader, Baldur von Schirach. Over 50,000 members of the Hitler Youth paraded before their Führer during the 1935 Party Congress. Hitler fully realized the importance of the various youth movements. Addressing the Hitler Youth on that occasion, Hitler emphasised the importance of their role in his new Germany; explaining how one day they would inherit everything that the Party was then creating.

60. *Reverse reads:* **Rally of Freedom. The youth - the new drummers of the nation.**
Boys from the various youth organizations, the *Deutsche Jungvolk* (German Young People; boys aged ten to fourteen years) and the *Hitler Jugend* (Hitler Youth; boys aged fourteen to eighteen years) attending the 1935 Party Rally. Some 54,000 members of the Hitler Youth took part in the 1935 *Reichsparteitag*. The Hitler Youth had been established in 1933 as a means of educating the young in the ways of National Socialism. By 1935 over 60 per cent of German youth, both male and female, belonged to one or other of the Nazi youth organizations.

61. Uncaptioned.
Commemorative Postmark Reads: **Party Congress of the NSDAP in Nürnberg from 10 to 16 Sept. 1935.**
The Führer salutes members of the *Reichsarbeitsdienst* (RAD; State Labour Service) at the 1935 Nuremberg Rally. A law passed in June 1935 required every able-bodied male to serve a period of six months in the RAD. This was a direct effort to tackle the many years of high unemployment that had existed throughout Germany prior to the Nazis coming to power, and a prerequisite to rearmament. The RAD was a disciplined and classless organization. The Nazi leadership were of the view that, the men who shoulder shovels today will one day shoulder rifles.

Standing directly below Hitler, again with outstretched arm, is Dr Robert Ley, (1890-1945) head of the *Deutsche Arbeitsfront* (DAF; German Labour Front). The German Labour Front was established on 10 May 1933. The organization comprised all workers in the Reich; over twenty million workers. The intention of the DAF was to 're-establish social peace in the world of labour', and, of course, to win over the working class to the Nazi way of life. For the most part the organization proved a success, providing better working conditions and security of employment. On the right stands Rudolf Hess, Deputy Führer, beside Hess stands Dr Wilhelm Frick (1877-1946), Minister of the Interior. Frick drew up the Nuremberg Laws that were announced during the 1935 Party Rally – see introduction to 1935 rally.

62. *Reverse reads:* **The Party Congress in Nürnberg 1935. The Navy march-past on the Day of the Wehrmacht.**

This is an interesting image in many ways. The Führer, in this instance standing on a low wooden platform, takes the salute as members of the new German Navy march by. On the right of the platform, in dark uniform, is Admiral Erich Raeder, Commander in Chief of the Navy. Standing above and behind Hitler on the next level and dressed in white is Leni Riefenstahl. The previous year 1934, Riefenstahl, under Hitler's patronage, produced and directed the film; *Triumph des Willens* (Triumph of the Will). This was, and indeed still is considered a masterpiece in film-making. In the background, and dominating the tribune of the Zeppelin Field is the wooden eagle designed by Albert Speer. This enormous wooden eagle with a wingspan of over thirty metres was in place in time for the 1934 Party Congress. It was finally replaced by a huge gilded swastika set in a wreath in 1937 (see postcard number 102). On the left wing of the eagle we see cameramen using a ladder to film and photograph events below. Riefenstahl had used similar techniques the previous year when filming Triumph of the Will.

63. *Reverse reads:* **The work army. Party Congress 1935.**
Thousands of RAD men assemble on the Zeppelin Field. The symbol of the RAD, a shovel bearing a swastika with two ears of corn beneath, appears on top of the pillar. The wreaths at the base of the pillar and the positions of the men in the foreground would indicate that some form of commemorative ceremony is taking place. As previously mentioned, the *Reichsarbeitsdeinst* was a disciplined organization. Its members marched and performed drill to the same level as that of the army. Having served the compulsory six month period in the RAD, members then transferred straight into the armed services, where instead of shouldering shovels, they shouldered rifles.

64. *Reverse reads:* **Party Congress 1935. The work soldiers.**
Men of the RAD fall in before their Führer on the Zeppelin Field. In establishing the RAD the Nazi Party virtually solved Germany's dire unemployment problem, a situation that had existed for many years, almost overnight. Members of the RAD did farm work amongst other things. During the 1936 Party Congress Hitler announced that the number of unemployed had been reduced from six million to one million. This announcement to a nation that had suffered long term deprivation through years of unemployment certainly increased Hitler's popularity.

65. *Reverse reads:* **Reichsparteitag Nürnberg.**
The demonstration of the armed services on the Zeppelin Field. The Führer greets the Wehrmacht. In the background Minister of Defence von Blomberg and Prime Minister Hermann Göring.
Hitler salutes the armed services as they parade before him on the Zeppelin Field during the 1935 Party Rally. Standing on the extreme left of the image is Hermann Göring. Next to Göring stands Minister of Defence, Colonel-General Werner von Blomberg. Hitler appointed von Blomberg Supreme Commander of the Wehrmacht in May 1935. As such von Blomberg oversaw the process of German rearmament. Below the podium stand two rows of steel-helmeted SS men of the Leibstandarte-SS Adolf Hitler (Hitler's personal Bodyguard Regiment).

66. Uncaptioned. (*top right*)
The heads of all three branches of the Wehrmacht; Grand Admiral Erich Raeder (1876-1960) Commander in Chief of the Navy, Hermann Göring (1893-1946) Commander in Chief of the Air Force, and Colonel-General Werner von Blomberg, head of the German Army join Hitler on the podium as he reviews a drive past of armoured vehicles on the Zeppelin Field.

The vehicles are *Schwerer Panzerspähwagen* (heavy six-wheeled armoured reconnaissance cars). When employed as a *Waffenwagen* (weapons car) the vehicle carried a crew of four. The turret mounted one machine gun and one 2cm Kw.K cannon. When used as a *Funkwagen* (radio car) the defensive weaponry consisted of one 2cm Kw.K only. Additionally, when employed as *Funkwagen,* vehicles were then fitted with large frame antennae (see the vehicle closest to those standing on the podium).

67. Nürnberg. SA camp Langwasser.
This image offers a superb view of the SA campsite at the Langwasser, close to the Zeppelin Arena. This huge tented area provided accommodation for many thousands of SA and SS men in the build-up to the rallies. Nazi flags stand neatly in the foreground. The whole scene is one of frantic activity as the excitement of such a major event in the Nazi calendar takes hold of the participants.

79

Reichsparteitag 1936

The eighth Nuremberg Rally; *Der Parteitag der Ehre* (The Rally of Honour) ran from 8 to 14 September 1936. This Rally celebrated Germany's recent bloodless occupation of the demilitarized *Rheinland* (Rhineland) in March that year. The Locarno Pact, concluded on 16 October 1925, essentially an agreement between Britain, France and Germany, guaranteed the inviolability of the demilitarized area of the Rhineland. One of the effects of signing the Locarno Pact was Germany's admission to the League of Nations in 1926. Germany retained political control of the Rhineland with its heavy industry under the terms of the Versailles Treaty. However, the conditions of the treaty clearly stated that German troops would not enter the demilitarized zone. Nazi Germany gave notice of their intention to withdraw from the League of Nations on 21 October 1933. On 8 March 1935 Germany denounced the Lacarno Pact. On 21 October 1935, exactly two years to the day after Germany's announcement of their intention to withdraw, Germany ceased to be a member of the League of Nations.

Nonetheless, Hitler knew he risked much as he tested the resolve of the western Allies when he ordered German troops into the Rhineland on 7 March 1936. Such a move was a direct violation of the Versailles Treaty. Again, as in 1935, when the Führer had announced the existence of the new German *Luftwaffe* to the world, there was little reaction. Yet again, the inaction of the Allies on this occasion only served to bolster Hitler's

68. *Reverse reads:* **Festival postcard. Party Congress of the NSDAP.**
Nürnberg 8-14 September 1936.
Just one example of a number of postcards designed to promote and advertise the eighth Party Congress of the Nazi Party in 1936. In this instance a Nazi eagle sits on a column with a silhouette of Nuremberg Castle in the background.

already growing confidence. In effect the occupation of the Rhineland was another psychological step along the road to Germany's complete abandonment of the Versailles Treaty. The inaction of the Allies in both the aforementioned instances, apart from a number of paper protests, would have long-reaching catastrophic effects. Commenting on events following the occupation of the Rhineland Hitler said; *'The forty-eight hours after the march into the Rhineland were the most nerve-racking of my life. If the French had then marched into the Rhineland, we would have had to withdraw with our tails between our legs, for the military resources at our disposal would have been wholly inadequate for even moderate resistance'*.

The *Wehrmacht;* the collective name for all three branches of the German armed forces; the Army, the Navy, and the Air Force, paraded en masse before their Führer at the 1936 *Reichsparteitag*. During one particular display by the *Luftwaffe,* seventeen aircraft flew in formation to form a swastika high in the sky over the rally grounds to the delight of the onlookers.

Hitler's rhetoric that year focused on the evils of Bolshevism, and how that 'mad bestial doctrine' threatened not only peace in Germany, but indeed Europe. Furthermore, Hitler stated that it was Germany, and Germany alone that stood as a bulwark against the spread of Bolshevism in the West. Addressing some 50,000 members of the Hitler Youth at the 1936 Party Congress Hitler told them; *'We live in exciting times. We make no complaints. We are used to battle, for out of it we came. We will plant our feet firmly on our earth, and no attack will move us. You will stand with me, should such a time come! You will stand before me, at my side, and behind me, holding our flags high! Let our old enemies attempt to rise up once more! They may wave their Soviet flags before us – but our flag will win the battle!'* The arena echoed to thunderous applause as the Führer ended his speech.

A second 'Four-Year Plan' intended to bring about German self-sufficiency in raw materials through further industrialization was announced at the 1936 *Reichsparteitag*. Hitler did not want Germany to be dependent on imported raw materials. The first 'Four-Year Plan' introduced in 1933 had successfully targeted the nation's high unemployment and economic problems. Interestingly, both plans were overseen by Hermann Göring, head of the *Luftwaffe*.

69. *Reverse reads:* **Festival postcard. Party Congress of the N.S.D.A.P. in Nürnberg 8-14 September 1936.**
The second postcard to be produced in the so-called 'Red Card' series designed to promote the 1936 Party Congress. The theme of this rally; *Der Parteitag der Ehre* (The Rally of Honour) celebrated Germany's recent peaceful occupation of the demilitarized Rhineland in March that year. This postcard and the preceding one, number 68, were designed by Prof. Richard Klein.

70. Uncaptioned.
This postcard bears no text whatsoever, even the reverse has no information relating to the photographer or the publisher. Nonetheless, this is a rare and very interesting image, for it shows members of the Protestant Church taking part in a Nazi parade through the streets of Nuremberg. Since the large banner in the background displays the coat of arms for the city of Nuremberg it is probably fair to assume that the photograph was taken during *Reichsparteitag*.

The clergyman in the front row on the left is the Bishop of Dresden, Friedrich Coch, the NSDAP Gau (District) consultant on church matters after 1933. The clergyman in the centre of the second row is Bishop Ludwig Müller. Müller was appointed 1st Reich Bishop in late 1933; as such he was Hitler's advisor on Protestant Church affairs. Both men were Nazi sympathizers.

The left side of the street is lined by lads from *Deutsches Jungvolk* (German Young People); a youth organization for boys aged ten to fourteen. Behind these lads are members of the general public while the right hand side of the street is lined with SA men.

71. Nürnberg. Hotel Deutscher Hof – Dwelling of the Führer.
When in Nuremberg, Hitler would stay at the Deutscher Hof. Situated at Frauentorgraben 29, the hotel was close to the Hauptbahnhof (Main Station). This postcard shows the hotel following the construction of the large extension in 1936. This extension is seen on the right of the image. Prior to the building of the extension the Führer stayed in a large room on the first floor overlooking the main road, just below where we see the two large flags on the front of the building. Hitler would review the many march-pasts on the road below from the windows. After 1936 the Führer was accommodated in the new extension. Thereafter, Hitler reviewed the march-pasts from the specially constructed balcony seen on the right.

72. The Hotel Deutscher Hof photographed in 2010. Over seventy years have passed since the previous photograph number 71 was taken. As we can see the windows have been replaced and the balcony used by Hitler to review the march-pasts has been removed. While a number of structural alterations have been carried out certain features remain unchanged and the building is still recognizable. The Deutscher Hof has been closed for a number of years; however, there are currently plans for this historic building.

73. Nürnberg. Our Führer in Hotel Deutscher Hof.
Hitler stands on the specially constructed balcony of the newly extended Hotel Deutscher Hof. His personal standard attached to the wall above flanked by the symbols of National Socialism. Two SS soldiers stand guard before the entrance while a number of high-ranking SS officers are observed on the left. Nuremberg, the spiritual centre of National Socialism was immersed in a sea of red as thousands of flags and banners were brought out during the annual Party Congress.

74. The same scene photographed in 2010. Obviously a number of structural changes have taken place. Nonetheless, this photograph shows the extension to Hotel Deutscher Hof completed in 1936. The balcony on which we saw Hitler standing in the previous image, number 73, stood above the doors directly opposite.

75. Uncaptioned.
Members of the *Hitlerjugend* (Hitler Youth) parade before their Führer. Standing beneath his personal standard, Hitler returns the salute as he reviews the march-past from the balcony of the Hotel Deutscher Hof above. With Hitler on the balcony is Reich Youth Leader, Baldur von Schirach.

76. Nürnberg, the city of the Reichsparteitag, Zeppelin Field – Honour Tribune.
The Ehrentribune on the Zeppelinfeld photographed in 1936. This postcard shows the Ehrentribune at a transitional stage. At this point the earlier large wooden eagle that dominated the centre of the structure behind the speaker's rostrum as seen in postcard number 45 (during the 1934 *Reichsparteitag*), and again in postcard number 62 (during the 1935 *Reichsparteitag*) has been removed. The wooden eagle would be replaced by an enormous gilded swastika set in a gilded wreath. Looking at the postcard we can see that a large wreathed swastika has been placed high on the end wall of the column on the left of the image. This was repeated on the column at the opposite end of the structure. Eventually two large cauldrons would be placed on top of these columns above the aforementioned swastikas. These huge cauldrons would be lit for added dramatic effect during night-time gatherings on the Zeppelin Field.

77. Uncaptioned.
Hitler salutes members of the RAD on the Zeppelin Field during a march-past at the 1936 Party Congress. Standing beside Hitler's Mercedes convertible is Konstantin Hierl (1875-1955), Head of the *Deutsche Arbeitsfront* (German Labour Front). This postcard was posted in Nuremberg on 10 September 1936; two days after the rally began.

78. The call to duty on the Zeppelin Field. Party Congress 1936.
One of the many night-time mass gatherings held on the Zeppelin Field. Again the whole scene is illuminated with Speer's mesmerizing *'Licht Dom'* (Cathedral of Light) effect. This is yet another postcard showing the Tribune during the aforementioned transitional stage, for Speer's large wooden eagle (see postcard number 62) is no longer in place, and, as yet, the later large gilded swastika set in a wreath that replaced it is not yet in place.

79. Uncaptioned.
Hitler, bare-headed, waits to step up to the microphones. Below, assembled on the Zeppelin Field, the massed ranks of SA and the SS stand in silence. Searchlights directed straight up into the night sky add to the drama. The Führer then delivered a speech that took the listeners on an emotional roller-coaster. Such was the power of Hitler's oratory. These words, or something along similar lines, would be how such an event might have been reported in the press or on the radio at the time. Small wonder therefore that the vast majority of the public were swept along in the highly-charged atmosphere of the Nuremberg Rallies.

80. Uncaptioned.
While uncaptioned, this absolutely superb image shows units of the German Armed Forces gathered before the Führer on the Zeppelinfeld during the 1936 Party Rally. Highly mechanized, the German Army was undoubtedly the most modern army in Europe at the time. It was as a result of this high level of mechanization, and therefore great manoeuvrability, that Hitler's forces swept aside all opposition during the early years of the Second World War.

The vehicles in the foreground are towing *Panzerabwehrkanone;* abbreviated 'PaK' 35/36 L/45 anti-tank guns. The armoured vehicles in the background are *Leichter Panzerspähwagen;* abbreviated le.Pz.Spw. light armoured reconnaissance cars. The model seen is the Sd.Kfz. 222 *Kanonenwagen* (gun car). Armament consisted of one turret mounted 2cm KwK 38L/55 cannon and one MG34 machine gun. The vehicle had a three man crew. The type saw extensive use in the reconnaissance role, particularly in Western Europe during the Second World War.

High above the speaker's rostrum in the background people can be seen standing on top of the structure. This is where the huge gilded swastika would be placed in time for the 1937 *Reichsparteitag.* The Zeppelinfeld would be the only structure ever to be fully completed at the rally grounds.

81. Nürnberg. National Party Rally Grounds. Luitpold Arena with Congress Hall.
This wonderful aerial photograph shows the Luitpold Arena in its entirety. In the foreground we see the terraces. The Luitpold Arena could accommodate 150,000 people. It was here on the speaker's rostrum, located in front of the three large banners on the upper left, that Hitler addressed the gathered masses, the SA and the SS. It was here that Hitler observed military manoeuvres and here where various other Nazi organizations performed before the Führer. The *Straße des Führers* (the Führer's Way) running through the centre of the image links the speaker's rostrum and the Ehrenhalle at its opposite end. On the left of the image we see part of the Congress Hall. Virtually nothing of the Luitpold Arena remains, only the Ehrenhalle (War Memorial) remains standing.

82. *Reverse reads:* **Nürnberg – City of the Party Congress. Luitpold Arena. The path of the Führer with a view of the monument to the dead. Führer's rostrum on the right. Architect: General Building Inspector Prof. Albert Speer.**
This postcard shows the paved walkway leading from the speaker's rostrum to the Ehrenhalle opposite. It was along this walkway that Hitler, accompanied initially by Ernst Röhm (see postcard number 15), then later together with Heinrich Himmler and Viktor Lutze (see postcards numbers 29 and 30) would walk solemnly, and silently to the Ehrenhalle. Once there they would pay their respects to the fallen while thousands of SA and SS men looked on.

83. Conference of the National Socialist Women's Organizations. Party Congress 1936.
Members of the *Frauenschaft* (Women's Organization) from all over the Reich gather in the Congress Hall during the 1936 Party Congress. The *N.S. Frauenschaft* came into being in 1933 following Hitler's coming to power. The organization was set up to teach Nazi ideals to German women and girls. They taught everything that was considered to be important from a National Socialist viewpoint. Everything from motherhood and domestic affairs to business matters was covered. It was compulsory for all women aged 18 to 30 to join the organization.

84. Women's Organization conference in the Conference Hall. *(top right)*
This postcard depicts a veritable who's who of the Nazi leadership. Working left to right we see; Adolf Hitler; Rudolf Hess, Deputy Führer; Heinrich Himmler, Reichsführer SS; Dr Wilhelm Frick, Reich Minister of the Interior; Dr Joseph Goebbels, Reich Minister for Public Enlightenment and Propaganda; and Martin Bormann, at that time Chief of Staff to Deputy Führer, Rudolf Hess.
 The lady in the photograph is Gertrud Scholtz-Klink (1902-1999). A member of the Nazi Party since the late 1920s, Scholtz-Klink held a number of important posts, amongst them head of the women's section of the *Deutsche Arbeitsfront* (DAF; German Labour Front). All have gathered in the Congress Hall close to the Luitpold Arena for a meeting of the National Socialist *Frauenschaft* organization where Hitler will address a female audience drawn from all corners of the Reich.

85. National Socialist Women's Organization Conference. *(below)*
Having already enjoyed musical entertainment provided by the orchestra in the foreground Adolf Hitler mounts the speaker's rostrum to address a hushed female audience in the Conference Hall during the 1936 Party Rally. Looking down the central aisle leading from the rostrum to the doors at the opposite end of the hall it appears that every end of row seat is occupied by a uniformed member of the SS. Having finished his speech, Hitler would have left the building using the central aisle. Enjoying as he did the adoration of the vast majority of German women Hitler would have needed protection as he left the hall, hence the need for the SS to hold back the over excited audience as the Führer made his exit.

Nürnberg. Zeltlager der S.A.

86. Camp of the S.A.
A superb aerial view of the huge SA camp that was located southeast of the rally grounds. Many thousands of SA, SS, and HJ, together with members of the other Nazi organizations were accommodated in this 'tented village' in the lead up to, and during the Party Congress each year. Postcard number 143 shows the location of the SA camp in relation to other structures on the rally grounds. The camp, referred to by the German word 'LAGER', is seen on the upper left of the image, in the area above the Märzfeld. The Märzfeld is shown as number 12 on the plan.

From 1939 sections of the camp were used to accommodate prisoners-of-war. As many as 30,000 prisoners from various nations were held there. The prisoners were employed by the City of Nuremberg and worked on various construction sites at the Party Rally Grounds until 1943. Many prisoners died due to a lack of food and the inadequate accommodation in the camp.

87. Nürnberg. Model of the Congress Building. *Reverse reads:* **City of the Reichsparteitag – Nürnberg. Party Rally Grounds. Model of the Congress Building, view from the east.**
Capacity: 50,000 people. Outer Area: 275 x 260m. Total Height: 80m. Completion Date: 1943.
This architectural model shows the Congress Hall that was to be constructed at the *Reichsparteitag-Gelände* (National Party Day Rally Grounds) at Nuremberg. The plans for this enormous building, the largest from the Third Reich period to remain standing in Germany, were drawn up by Nuremberg architects, Ludwig and Franz Ruff. The foundation stone for the never-to-be-completed Congress Hall was laid in 1935.

The design of the Congress Hall is undoubtedly reminiscent of the ancient Coliseum in Rome. In 1973 the Congress Hall was designated a listed building. This means that the City of Nuremberg is responsible for the maintenance of the former Congress Hall. Since November 2001 the *Dokumentationszentrum Reichsparteitags-Gelände* (Documentation Centre National Party Day Rally Grounds) has occupied the north wing of this monumental building.

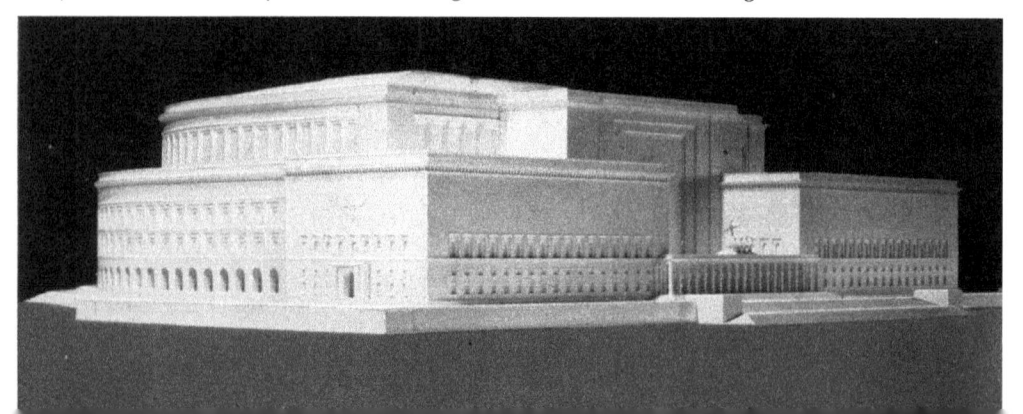

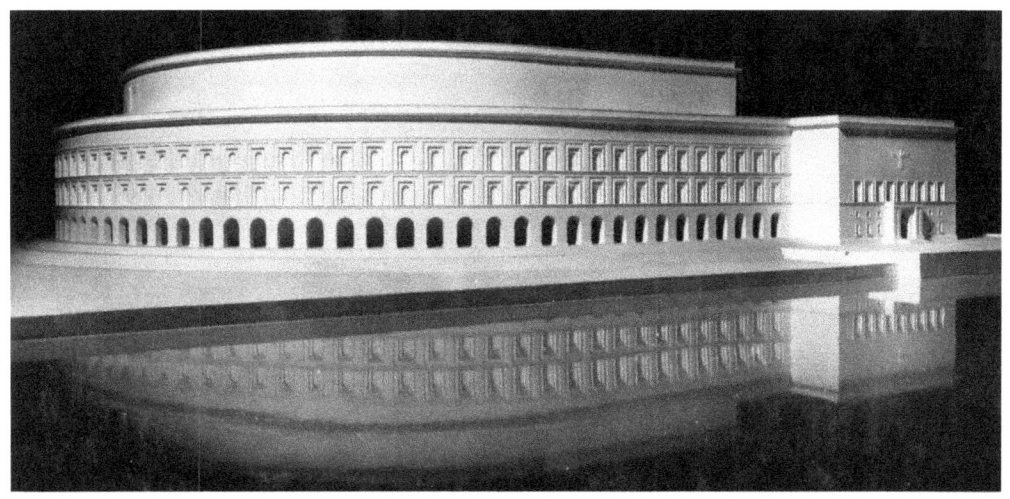

88. Congress Building Nürnberg. *Reverse reads:* **City of the Reichsparteitag Nürnberg. Certified model admission from the Führer; approved for the execution of the determined draft.**
Another model of Nuremberg architect's, Ludwig and Franz Ruff's planned Congress Hall. A huge roof with no underpinning had been planned to cover the interior court that, when finished, would have accommodated 50,000 people. The partially completed building stands close to the Dutzendteich Lake (see postcard number 143 for the location of the Congress Hall; number 5 on the plan.)

89. Congress Building Nürnberg. *Reverse reads:* **City of the Reichsparteitag Nürnberg. Certified model admission from the Führer; approved for the execution of the determined draft.**
This marvellous postcard shows the interior of the Congress Hall as it would have appeared had the project been completed. Again this is a photograph of one of the many architectural models that were produced. Nonetheless it certainly helps to convey an impression of the scale of the vast interior that would have accommodated 50,000 delegates.

90. The *Congressbau* (Congress Building) as photographed in 2010. This photograph was taken from a point on the *Großestraße*, looking back at the building across the now dried up Dutzendteich, and from an angle similar to that seen in postcard number 88. In years past the former Congress Building has been a concert venue and storage facility.

91. The *Großestraße* (Great Road) photographed in 2010. The *Großestraße* was to be the central axis, when completed it would connect the major buildings located on the Party Rally Grounds. Looking at postcard number 143, the *Großestraße* is the road running through the Dutzenteich connecting the Austellungsbau (number 7, bottom right) with the Märzfeld (number 12, top centre). The *Großestraße* was to be 2,000 metres long and 60 metres wide. Of the intended 2,000 metre length, only 1,500 metres were completed. Some 60,000 large granite slabs formed the surface of the completed area. Running as it does from the Märzfeld in a north-westerly direction, the Great Road points towards Nuremberg Castle. This again was a deliberate attempt by the Nazis to create a link; a relationship between the Third Reich and Nuremberg's important medieval past.

Reichsparteitag 1937

The ninth Nuremberg Rally; *Der Parteitag der Arbeit* (The Rally of Labour) celebrated the successful reduction of unemployment throughout Germany under the Nazi regime. At the beginning of 1933 Germany had six million unemployed. The Nazis managed to reduce this figure year on year. By 1939 the number of those unemployed stood at just over 300,000. The 1937 rally ran from 6 to 13 September. An anti-Semitic book entitled, *Der Ewige Jude* (The Eternal Jew) published by *Eher Verlag,* the Nazi Party's publishing house in Munich was released that year. *Der Ewige Jude* consisted of 265 photographs accompanied by brief captions. The book's aim was to portray the Jews as undesirables.

Dr Joseph Goebbels, Minister for Public Enlightenment and Propaganda, launched several scathing attacks against the Jews during speeches he made at the 1937 rally. While Robert Ley, head of the *Deutsche Arbeitsfront* (DAF; German Labour Front) praised Hitler, saying; 'Everything comes from Adolf Hitler. His faith is our faith, and therefore our daily prayer is: "I believe in Adolf Hitler alone!"' Rarely has a politician enjoyed such an accolade.

Festliches Nürnberg (Festival Nuremberg) a short documentary film with a running time of just over twenty minutes is a compilation of footage from both the 1936 and 1937 *Reichsparteitage.* The film was directed by Hans Weidemann (1904-1975) who worked for the film department of the Propaganda Ministry. Festival Nuremberg was released in 1937. The film is

92. *Reverse reads:* **Festival postcard. Party Congress of the NSDAP in Nürnberg 6-13 September 1937.**
One of a number of postcards designed to promote and advertise the ninth Party Congress of the Nazi Party in 1937.
This postcard was designed by Prof. Richard Klein. In this case Klein's Nazi eagle dominates the image while Nazi banners form the background.

notable for the fact that it includes footage of Albert Speer's inspired 'Cathedral of Light' lighting effect; this was filmed on the evening of 10 September 1937 on the Zeppelin Field. It has been said that *Festliches Nürnberg* picks up where Leni Riefenstahl's *Triumph des Willens* leaves off.

His Imperial Highness, Prince Chichibu Yasuhito of Japan, brother of then Japanese Emperor, Showa, attended the 1937 Nuremberg Rally as part of a European tour that year. During his visit Prince Chichibu met Adolf Hitler in Nuremberg Castle for talks aimed at bringing their two countries closer together. It is said that the Prince returned to Japan absolutely convinced that the German Führer was indeed a great politician. At the same time however, the Prince retained some reservations regarding Hitler's expressed views towards Soviet Russia.

The Führer delivered nine speeches during the 1937 *Reichsparteitag*. The importance of the Nuremberg Rallies to the Nazi movement cannot be underestimated, for they were as much a venue for making announcements to Germany and the rest of the world as they were a place to demonstrate the bonds between the leader and his followers. The last day of the rally was 'Armed Forces Day', when Hitler, having reviewed the army then watched a number of displays and military manoeuvres carried out on the Zeppelinfeld.

Not surprisingly, the Nazi Party published a series of books dedicated to the *Reichsparteitage* between 1933 and 1938. Each volume was a detailed record of the most recent rally. These books are generally referred to as the 'Guide Books' and, occasionally, the 'Red Books' due to their red covers. While each contains a number of photographs taken at that year's rally, more importantly every book contains the entire text of Hitler's speeches from that particular rally alongside those of other leading Nazis speaking at the event. Made available soon after each *Reichsparteitag*, the 'Guide Books' give a detailed account of the event and brought the words of the Führer to those unable to attend the rally.

Another series of books published by the Nazi Party covering the Nuremberg Rallies are the 'Yearbooks', sometimes referred to as the 'Blue Books', again due to the colour of the covers. While intentionally produced to target the masses, these 'Yearbooks' concentrate on presenting a photographic record of the event, therefore the accompanying text is much less than that contained the aforementioned 'Guide Books'.

Additionally, the *Völkischer Beobachter* (VB; Nationalist Observer) the official Nazi Party newspaper printed Hitler's speeches from the Nuremberg Rallies in full, together with the speeches of the other Nazi leaders. Another series of books entitled; *Reden des Führers* (Speeches of the Führer) include additional speeches delivered by Hitler to

93. Reverse reads: **Festival postcard. Congress of the N.S.D.A.P. in Nürnberg 6-13 September 1937.** The third postcard to be produced in the so-called 'Red Card' series designed to promote the 1937 Party Congress. The theme of this rally; *Der Parteitag der Arbeit* (The Rally of Labour) celebrated the dramatic reduction in unemployment throughout Germany under the Nazi regime. Again this postcard was designed by Prof. Richard Klein.

various groups and at different venues. While Heinrich Hoffmann, both Hitler's personal and official Party photographer, also produced books showcasing the rallies through his many photographs.

In October 1937 and amid some controversy, the Duke of Windsor (formerly King Edward VIII) and his wife (formerly Mrs Wallis Simpson) visited Germany. Crowned Edward VIII on 20 January 1936, the king took the decision to abdicate on 11 December later that same year. The King had been forced to choose between the Crown and his love for Mrs Simpson, an American divorcee. Edward followed his heart and the couple were married in France on 3 June 1937. How times change. That the king could marry a commoner and a divorcee was deemed totally unacceptable in 1936. Today it is quite apparent that these rules no longer apply. While Edward was, to quite an extent vilified by members of the British royal family because of his views on Hitler and the Nazis, research into the activities of other members of the extended family throughout Europe at this time also makes for dark reading.

94. Arrival of the Führer in Nürnberg. *Reverse reads:* **Party Congress Nürnberg 1937.**
Having just landed at Nuremberg, Hitler appears composed and self-assured as he walks away from his personal aircraft, a Junkers Ju52. The tri-engine Ju52 was introduced in 1932. Capable of carrying up to eighteen passengers the aircraft proved extremely reliable and was used by national airlines the world over. During the Second World War the Luftwaffe employed the rugged Ju52 in a number of roles; from bomber, to military transport, to air-ambulance.

The Führer is accompanied by Heinrich Himmler (1900-1945). Himmler became head of the SS in 1929. In 1934 Himmler acquired control of the *Sicherheitsdienst 'SD'* (SS Security Service) and the *Geheime Staatspolizei 'Gestapo'* (Secret State Police) the same year. By 1936 all German Police were under Himmler's control. On the extreme right, and standing under the wing of the aircraft is Rudolf Hess, Deputy Führer.

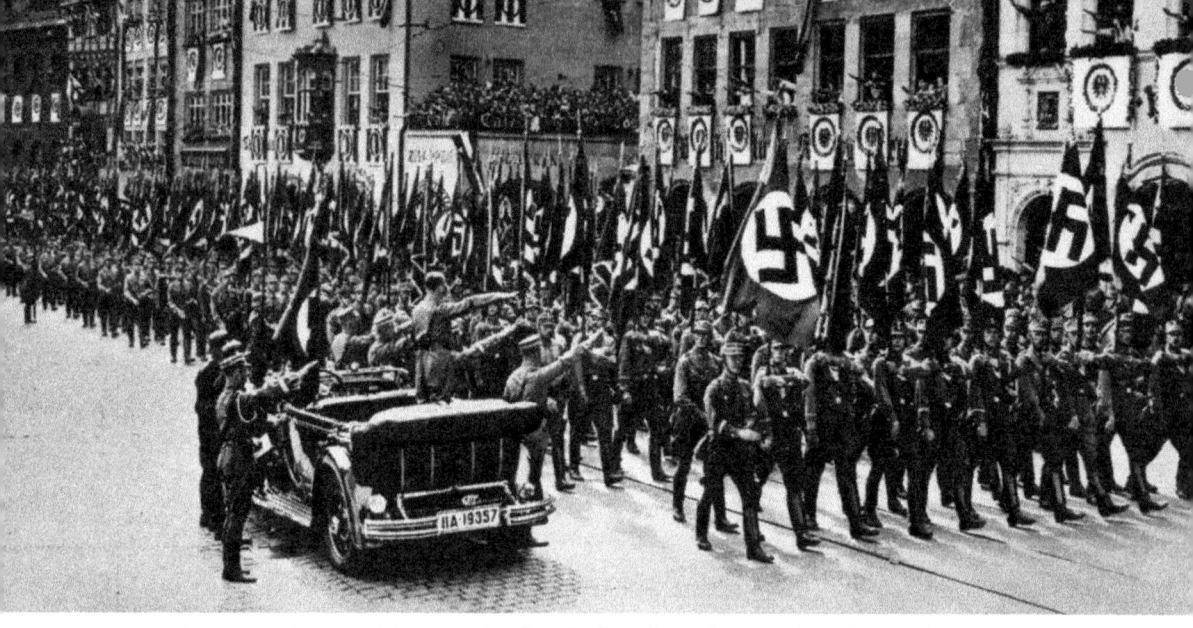

95. Nürnberg: March-past of the organizations before the Führer on the Adolf-Hitler-Platz.
The massed ranks of the SA parade before the Führer in the centre of Nuremberg. From every window of every building people can be seen saluting the marching columns. The enthusiasm for these *Reichsparteitage* of the mid 1930s knew no bounds. People travelled from all corners of the Reich to attend these enormous annual events. The enthralling spectacular of *Reichsparteitag* also attracted numerous foreign visitors to Nuremberg each September.

96. March-past of the HJ (Hitler Youth) before the Führer.
Members of the Hitler Youth salute the Führer as they march past the Hotel Deutscher Hof during the 1937 Party Congress. Standing on the balcony with Hitler are; Deputy Führer, Rudolf Hess (centre), and Hitler Youth Leader, Baldur von Schirach (right). Thousands of people line the streets below. The Deutscher Hof stands just outside Nuremberg's ancient city walls.

97. *Reverse reads:* **Party Congress Nürnberg 1937.**
Torchlight procession of the political leaders: March-past before the Führer at the Deutscher Hof.
Torch-lit night-time processions were popular Nazi activities. In this instance we see political leaders from all over the Reich parading before their Führer. Hitler, standing on the balcony of the Hotel Deutscher Hof is picked out by a spotlight overhead. There can be little doubt that the sight of thousands of men in uniform marching silently through the streets carrying flags and torches contributed a high level of mystique to the proceedings. Drama, ceremony, ritual, these factors were never overlooked during the planning any major Nazi event.

98. March-past of the political leaders before the Führer.
Another superb image showing Hitler standing on the balcony of the Hotel Deutscher Hof as he salutes thousands of torch-bearing men marching along the street below. On the left of the image, behind the hanging swastika banners we can see part of Nuremberg's old city walls. The large Gothic style building in the background on the left is the Germanisches Nationalmuseum (Germanic Museum). This building was badly damaged during the Second World War and no longer exists in its original form.

99. *Reverse reads:* **Party Congress Nürnberg 1937.**
The Führer goes to the Party Congress.
Hitler climbs the steps leading to the Congress Hall adjacent to the Luitpold Arena during the 1937 Party Congress. Amongst Hitler's entourage are; second from left; Martin Bormann, Chief of Staff to Deputy Führer, Rudolf Hess, directly behind Hitler is; Heinrich Himmler, Reichsführer SS, and directly behind Himmler is; Joachim von Ribbentrop, Ambassador to Great Britain, after February 1938 Reich Minister for Foreign Affairs. Men of the Leibstandarte-SS Adolf Hitler (Hitler's personal Bodyguard Regiment) form the guard of honour in the background.

The Ehrenhalle (War Memorial) is seen on the upper right of the image with the *Straße des Führers* (the Führer's Way) the paved walkway that connected the Ehrenhalle with the Führer's rostrum running right to left across the parade ground. On this occasion the public stands in the background are empty; these would be filled to capacity when events were held in the Luitpold Arena.

100. Roll-call of the SA, SS, NSKK and NSFK in the Luitpold Arena.
With his personal standard placed to the right of the speaker's rostrum, Adolf Hitler addresses the massed ranks of the SA, the SS, the NSKK (see caption number 50) and the NSFK; *Nationalisozialistisches Fliegerkorps* (National Socialist Flying Corps) a special aircraft unit of the NSDAP in the Luitpold Arena. The stands in the foreground are packed with men wearing the uniforms of the various branches of the services and the Party together with members of the public.

101. Nürnberg, the city of the Reichsparteitage. Zeppelin Meadow.
This postcard shows the Zeppelinfeld virtually completed. The large wooden eagle seen above the Tribune in postcards numbers 45 and 62 is gone. In its place on top of the Tribune we can just make out the framework built to assist in the installation of the huge gilded swastika and wreath that would replace it. This would see work on the Zeppelinfeld, the only structure at the *Reichsparteitag-Gelände* (Nazi Party Day Rally Grounds) to be completed, at an end. Albert Speer found his inspiration for the design of the Tribune on the Zeppelinfeld in the Pergamon Altar. The altar, build in the 2nd Century BC, had been discovered by German archaeologist, Karl Humann (1839-1896) in 1878. Humann excavated the altar between 1878 and 1886. In 1902 the Pergamon Altar was shipped to Berlin where it was reconstructed in the Pergamon Museum. The altar has been described as the finest piece of Hellenistic art ever discovered.

102. Nürnberg, Reichsparteitag Rally Grounds: Honour Tribune on the Zeppelinfeld.
This image reveals the completed Tribune on the Zeppelin Field with the enormous gilded swastika set in its huge wreath in position on top of the structure. One of the two huge cauldrons that were lit during the night-time parades and gatherings held on the Zeppelin Field can be seen on top of the end wall of the Tribune on the left. Nazi drapes, each several metres long, hang between the columns in the background. Dwarfed by the scale of the Tribune, people wander around awestruck. This was, of course, part of the intention, to raise the credibility and importance of the regime in the public view.

103. Nürnberg. Reichsparteitag Rally Grounds. Zeppelin Field.
This absolutely superb aerial photograph shows the Zeppelin Field in its entirety. All thirty-four towers, each bearing six flagpoles are clearly visible. The Tribune and grandstands around the field were completed in 1936. The white building at the top of the image was a transformer building housing electrical installations. This had been constructed to provide the additional electric power necessary for, and sources differ on the number, anything from 120 to 150 anti-aircraft searchlights used to produce Speer's 'Cathedral of Light' effect during the many night-time parades. The grey area to the left is the Dutzendteich Lake. Close examination of this image reveals railway lines and indeed a train close to the top right hand corner. A small station, Bahnhof Dutzendteich, located adjacent to the Zeppelin Field Tribune was rebuilt in 1934 in an effort to improve transport links with the nearby city.

104. Uncaptioned.
The Führer, having mounted the speaker's rostrum in the Zeppelin Field addresses the perfectly formed ranks of the RAD at the 1937 Party Congress. It would appear that every detail relating to the positioning of the various groups on the field has been accomplished with typical German efficiency. The Party Congress provided an opportunity to strengthen the bond between the Führer and his audience, regardless as to which of the many Nazi organizations were assembled before him. Typically, Hitler tailored his speeches so that they were always relevant to a particular audience's activities and interests.

Again, Hitler, contrary to most of today's politicians, wrote all his own speeches. To the annoyance of his secretaries, Hitler would leave the dictation of speeches to the last minute. His reasoning for this was that things changed constantly, therefore by leaving the dictation to the last possibly moment, his speech would always be up to date, and, if necessary, would only ever require minimal alteration.

105. Nürnberg the city of the Party Congress. Entrance to Zeppelin Field.
This entrance to the Zeppelin Field can also be seen in postcard number 103. If we look at the right hand side of postcard 103 we can see this same end of wall column in the distance. In this instance we are afforded a close-up view of the column with the ubiquitous swastika and wreath attached. A cauldron is mounted on top of the column; an identical column stands at the other end of the Tribune. During night-time parades these cauldrons were lit to add dramatic effect. Surprisingly the cauldrons have survived. While one is currently housed inside the Tribune building itself, the other is stored close to the nearby Franken Stadium.

106. The same scene photographed in 2010. In comparing this photograph with the previous image, postcard number 105, we can see that the pillared galleries in the background where the large Nazi banners once hung have been removed. These were taken down in 1967 for safety reasons, it was thought that the pillars were deteriorating; they had become structurally unsound and were considered dangerous. Again the tops of the end walls where the cauldrons once stood, as observed in postcard 105, were lowered to about half their previous height in the mid 1970s for the same reasons.

107. Nürnberg. Zeppelin Field with Festival Tribune.
This photograph provides a close-up view of one of the thirty-four towers and embankments that together formed the perimeter of the Zeppelin Field. The six steel flagpoles on top of every tower provided for the flying of a total of 204 large Nazi flags. In the foreground we can see some of the steps that led up the 6.5 meter high embankments to the spectator's terraces overlooking the parade ground. In the background the huge wreathed swastika that crowns the completed Tribune shines in the sun. Directly below that stands the speaker's rostrum with Nazi banner attached.

108. Uncaptioned.
Hitler stands before the microphones on the Tribune at the Zeppelin Field during a night-time rally. The Führer's personal standard is visible on the rostrum behind him. The silhouette of the men in uniform against the illuminated wall in the background creates a menacing impression. On the left of the image we can see cameramen at work recording the event. On top of the wall above the cameramen we see one of the aforementioned cauldrons (see postcard number 105) alight. The background reveals pillars of light reaching high up into the night sky; part of Speer's inspired 'Cathedral of Light' effect.

109. The same scene photographed in 2010. This photograph reveals how the structure has been altered through the years. In comparing it with the previous image, postcard number 108, we can see that the end wall where the cauldron once stood has been removed. Additionally, the columns that connected the end wall to the main part of the Tribune behind where Hitler is seen standing in the previous image have also been removed. Furthermore, the metal guardrail on the speaker's rostrum has been replaced.

110. Model of the German Stadium.
Reverse reads: **Nürnberg City of the Party Congress. Model of the German Stadium.**
Date of laying the foundation stone: 9.9.1937.
Capacity: 405,000 people. Inner Area: 150 by 380m.
Height: Corner Towers: 100m. Height of Outer Walls around 85m.
Presumed Completion Date: 1943.

An architectural model of Albert Speer's German Stadium that was to be constructed at the rally grounds. Speer, using the ancient Circus Maximus in Rome and the stadium at Olympia as his inspiration, drew up plans for the world's largest sports stadium. Adolf Hitler laid the foundation stone at a ceremony on 9 September 1937. As the postcard shows, the German Stadium was to be a horseshoe-shaped structure of monumental proportions. The playing area alone would cover 55,000 square metres (over 180,000 square feet). Work on the stadium came to a virtual halt when the Second World War began in late 1939, so that by 1945 only the excavation stage of this vast project had been carried out. Postcard number 143 shows the position of the planned German Stadium in relation to other structures at the Party Rally Grounds. The stadium is shown as number 11 on the plan.

111. *Reverse reads:* **As previous postcard, number 110.**
While taken from a different angle, this photograph of the same architectural model shows the colonnaded main entrance to the stadium in better detail. Intended to accommodate an audience of over 400,000 people the German Stadium, had it ever been completed, would have been colossal.

112. Labour Service – Girl's Camp.
This aerial photograph shows the Girl's Camp set up for the 1937 Party Congress. The exact location of the camp is unknown. The *Jungmädel* (Young Girls) organization came under the umbrella of the Hitler Youth movement. Girls aged ten to fourteen were expected to join the *Jungmädel*. On reaching fourteen they became members of the *Bund Deutscher Mädel* (BdM; League of German Girls) where they stayed until aged twenty-one. The sole purpose of these organizations was to indoctrinate members in the ways of National Socialism. On reaching the age of twenty-one these young ladies either entered the workplace or were expected to marry and become mothers.

113. *Reverse reads:* **Reichsparteitag. Camp of the Women's Labour Service.**
A group of ladies from the women's branch of the *Reichsarbeitsdienst* (RAD; State Labour Service) as already discussed in caption number 61. While the slogan; 'We want to ride to Ostland', (Ostland, referring to the Baltic States, Belarus, and Eastern Poland) seems rather curious, we can make out figures on horseback painted on the tent just behind the young lady standing on the left. Members of the various *Frauenschaften* (Women's Organizations) were also accommodated in tents during the annual *Reichsparteitag*. This particular group appear to keeping themselves well entertained.

114. Uncaptioned.
This postcard bears no information as to the photographer or the publisher. Nonetheless, it is an interesting image for all that. The photograph shows part of the *KdF-Stadt* (KdF-Town) completed in 1937. The complex stood at the north eastern end of the Rally grounds. This was a recreational area managed by the Nazi *KdF - Kraft durch Freude* (Strength through Joy) organization. These wooden buildings were used for the exhibition of regional products and events involving folklore and tradition by way of entertainment for those attending the Nazi Party Rallies. Most evenings these halls echoed to the sounds of drinking, music and dancing. In 1942 the wooden buildings of *KdF-Stadt* were destroyed during an air-raid.

115. *Reverse reads:* **City of the Party Congress Nürnberg. KdF Town – Berlin Hall.**
This wonderful postcard image shows the interior of one of the buildings discussed in the previous caption, number 114. This particular hall is the Berlin Hall, this is confirmed by the words 'Unter den Linden' appearing on the banner beneath the large picture on the opposite wall. There is a stage at the opposite end of the hall to accommodate the band, while the long tables arranged in orderly rows await the arrival of the hundreds of revellers who will fill the venue when the doors are flung open at the end of the day.

Reichsparteitag 1938

The tenth Nuremberg Rally; *Der Parteitag Großdeutschland* (The Rally of Greater Germany) celebrated the annexation of Austria to the German Reich six months earlier. This, the last of the great Nuremberg Rallies ran from 5 to 12 September 1938 and was attended by some 700,000 Nazi Party members representing various organizations within the NSDAP. Kurt von Schuschnigg, Austria's Federal Chancellor had tried to resist Hitler's demands regarding the annexation of his country. However, having been called to a meeting at Hitler's private residence, the Berghof near Berchtesgaden on 12 February 1938, and under immense pressure, von Schuschnigg was forced to lift the ban on Austrian Nazis and to appoint the pro-Nazi, Artur Seyss-Inquart, Minister of the Interior. This act sounded the death-knell for independent Austria. Seyss-Inquart, in his new capacity wasted no time in turning his country over to Hitler.

German troops crossed the Austrian border in a peaceful takeover on 12 March 1938. Less than a month later, the question of *Anschluss* (Union) between Austria and Germany was decided by ballot on 10 April 1938. In reality the question of *Anschluss* was already decided, nonetheless the Austrian population were asked to ratify the annexation in a free vote. The result was an overwhelming 'yes' to the question of 'union' with 99.7 per cent of the electorate voting in favour of the move.

Hitler, an Austrian by birth, had long wished to see his homeland joined to the German Reich. The Führer, who became a German citizen in 1932, wanted to forge an empire of German-speaking peoples. Alongside the annexation of Austria, this would later include other German territories lost when the map of Europe had been redrawn after the First World War. The Saarland, an area along the River Saar and bordering France had been lost after the First World War. This area, rich in coal, was administered by the League of Nations from 1919 until 1935. On 13 January 1935 a plebiscite showed 91 per cent of the region's population in favour of a return to Germany.

As already discussed, the demilitarized Rhineland had been occupied by German troops in March 1936. Hitler would then turn his attention to the Sudetenland in Czechoslovakia. Formerly Austrian territory, the Sudetenland was home to some three million German-speaking people. Konrad Henlein, leader of the *Sudeten Deutsche Partei* (Sudeten German Party), contrived, with the help of Nazi Germany to see the Sudetenland become part of the German Reich. The Munich Agreement, signed by Britain, France, Germany and Italy on the night of 29/30 September 1938, gave Hitler a free hand in the Sudetenland. The region was peacefully occupied by German troops on 1 October 1938. Again, the Memelland, part of Lithuania since the end of the First World War also returned to Germany on 23 March 1939, when this area was peacefully occupied by German troops.

Some 80,000 *Hitler Jugend* (HJ; Hitler Youth) paraded before their Führer at the 1938 *Reichsparteitag*. Having watched the HJ carry out military type manoeuvres Hitler spoke to those gathered saying; *'You, my youth, are our nation's most precious guarantee for a great future, and you are destined to become the leaders of a glorious new order under the supremacy of National Socialism. Never forget that one day you will rule the world!'*

116. *Reverse reads:* **Party Congress Nürnberg.**
Yet another striking image in postcard form used to advertise and promote the tenth Party Congress of the Nazi Party to be held in Nuremberg from 5-12 September 1938.

In this instance one of Kurt Schmid-Ehmen's magnificent bronze eagles situated in the Luitpold Arena dominates the foreground. In the background we look across the rooftops of the old city towards Nuremberg Castle.

Stirring words to impart to impressionable young men. It is small wonder then that many of these teenage lads later joined the army or the SS. At its height in 1939 the Hitler Youth claimed a membership of almost 7.5 million across the Reich.

Hitler used the occasion of the 1938 Party Congress symbolically. On his instructions, the symbols of the First Reich, the Imperial Crown, the Orb of Empire, the Sceptre, and the Imperial Sword were taken from Vienna, their resting place for 142 years, and brought back to Nuremberg, their original resting place and the spiritual centre of his own Third Reich. During the presentation of these venerated objects Hitler swore that thereafter they would remain in Nuremberg forever. In bringing the symbols of the Holy Roman Empire back to Nuremberg, Hitler was deliberately toying with the emotions of every citizen. Their sense of patriotism, of belonging, of duty, Hitler believed, would encourage them to follow the Nazi banner and bind them even more closely to him.

Much was expected from the Führer's closing speech on 12 September 1938, the final day of the Party Congress. Indeed the foreign correspondents attending the event and the countries they represented expected the worst. As he began speaking, Hitler talked at length about the Party's struggle through the early years. He then moved on to his condemnation of the Czechs saying; *'I am in no way willing that here in the heart of Germany a second Palestine should be permitted to arise. The poor Arabs are defenceless and deserted. The Germans in Czechoslovakia are neither defenceless nor are they deserted, and people should take note of that fact'.* He continued; *'We should be sorry if this were to disturb or damage our relations with other European states, but the blame does not lie with us!'* On reaching the end of this part of his address Hitler concluded; *'I have not demanded that 3.5 million Frenchmen or Englishmen be given over to German oppression. I have demanded that the oppression of 3.5 million Germans in Czechoslovakia must end, and that they must have the right of self determination'.* The Czechs, the English and the French had expected much worse. Even Mussolini on hearing the live radio broadcast of Hitler's speech replied; *'I had expected a more threatening speech. . . . Nothing is lost'.*

Within weeks of the Führer's speech the Czech crisis had reached boiling point. However, through skilful manoeuvring, Hitler completely outflanked his opponents and the Sudetenland question was peacefully resolved when the area became part of the Reich following the Munich Agreement. Nonetheless, few realized that the seeds of wrath that would ultimately lead to the Second World War had already been sown.

The running order of the programme for the 1938 Nazi Party Congress was as follows:

Monday 5 September: **Day of Greeting.**
Reception for the international press.
Welcome reception for Hitler's arrival at the *Rathaus* (City Hall).
Speakers: *Oberbürgermeister* (Lord Mayor) Willy Liebel and Adolf Hitler.

Tuesday 6 September: **Day of the Opening of the Nazi Party Congress.**
The Führer reviews the flags of the Hitler Youth.
Official opening of the Nazi Party Congress and the reading of Hitler's proclamation by Adolf Wagner.
Speakers: Rudolf Hess, Julius Streicher and Adolf Wagner.

117. *Reverse reads:* **Festival postcard. Party Congress of the NSDAP in Nürnberg 5-12 September 1938.**
The fourth postcard produced in the so-called 'Red Card' series; promoting the 1938 Party Congress. The theme of this rally; *Der Parteitag Großdeutschland* (The Rally of Greater Germany) celebrated the annexation of Austria on 12 March earlier that year.

This, the last of the Nuremberg Party Rallies was the largest ever held where 700,000 members of the various Nazi organizations took part in the week-long event. Again this postcard was designed by Prof. Richard Klein.

Presentation of the Imperial Regalia, including the Crown Jewels to Adolf Hitler.
Opening of the exhibition *'Kampf in Osten'* ('The Struggle in the East').
Speaker: Alfred Rosenberg.
Cultural meeting followed by the presentation of National Prizes for Art and Science.
Speakers: Alfred Rosenberg and Adolf Hitler.

Wednesday 7 September: **Day of the RAD; Reich Labour Service.**
Review of the Reich Labour Service on the Zeppelin Field.
Speakers: Konstantin Hierl and Adolf Hitler.
Parade of the Reich Labour Service through Nuremberg.
Continuation of the Nazi Party Congress.
Speakers: Alfred Rosenberg, Erich Hilgenfeldt and Adolf Wagner.

Thursday 8 September: **Day of Fellowship.**
Athletic Games.
Continuation of the Nazi Party Congress. Speakers: Dr Otto Dietrich and Dr Fritz Todt.
Political Leader's torchlight parade.

Friday 9 September: **Day of the Political Leaders.**
Continuation of the Nazi Party Congress. Speakers: Max Amann, Walter Darré and Konstantin Hierl.
Meeting of the Nazi Women's Association in the Luitpold Hall.
Speaker: Gertrude Scholtz-Klink.
Review of the Political Leaders on the Zeppelin Field.
Speakers: Robert Ley and Adolf Hitler.

Saturday 10 September: **Day of the Hitler Youth.**
Review of the Hitler Youth on the Zeppelin Field. Speakers: Rudolf Hess and Adolf Hitler.
Meeting of the committee of the *Deutsche Arbeitsfront* (DAF; German Labour Front).
Speakers: Robert Ley and Hermann Göring.
Final day of the athletic games.
Continuation of the Nazi Party Congress.
Speakers: Robert Ley, Fritz Reinhardt and Joseph Goebbels.

Sunday 11 September: **Day of the SA and SS.**
Mass meeting of the SA and the SS on the Zeppelin Field.
Speakers: Viktor Lutze and Adolf Hitler.
Parade through Nuremberg.
Meeting of the political leadership of the Nazi Party. Speaker: Rudolf Hess.

Monday 12 September: **Day of the Armed Forces.**
Review and mass meeting of the German Army. Speaker: Adolf Hitler.
Army manoeuvres on the Zeppelin Field.
Closing ceremony of the Nazi Party Congress. Speaker: Adolf Hitler.

118. *Reverse reads:* **'Greater Germany Reborn'. The Imperial Jewels in the Treasury in Vienna.**
This Hoffmann photograph shows four pieces of the Imperial Regalia of the Holy Roman Empire. The regalia consisted of a total of thirty-seven items. The most important of these were; the crown, the orb, the cross, the holy lance, the sceptre, and the sword. From 1424-1796 the regalia had been kept in the Church of the Holy Ghost in Nuremberg Castle. In 1796 and in view of the threat posed by Napoleon's advancing army, the regalia were moved, first to Regensburg where it was kept for four years, then on to Vienna where it would remain.

Within days of the annexation of Austria to the Third Reich, Hitler would have the symbolic Imperial Regalia returned to Nuremberg where it would be kept in the St Katharinenkirche (St Katharine's Church). The church was virtually destroyed by Allied bombing during the Second World War. Only the ruins remain today. The regalia are now housed in the Imperial Treasury in the Hofburg Palace in Vienna.

116

119. Nürnberg. Fleischbrücke with view towards Adolf-Hitler-Platz.
The old city festooned with Nazi flags and banners prepares for the Party Congress. The large rooftop in the distance is part of the St Sebalduskirche, the Lutheran Church. This was part of the route along which thousands of uniformed members of the various Nazi organizations; the SA, the SS and the HJ *Hitlerjugend* (Hitler Youth) marched on their way to the rally grounds. A little further along the street, before the St Sebalduskirche and on the right was the renamed Adolf-Hitler-Platz where the Führer would take the salute. This postcard was posted in Nuremberg on 8 September 1938 to an address in Vienna.

120. The same scene photographed in 2010. In comparing this image with the previous postcard, number 119, we can see how much the area has changed through the seventy odd years that have passed between photographs. However, certain features remain unaltered. In the foreground, on the left, the famous bull seen above the portal is still in place on the Fleischbrücke, and in the distance we can still see the roof of the St Sebalduskirche. The rebuilding necessitated following intensive wartime bombing has resulted in many changes to the buildings on both sides of the street.

117

121. The arrival of the Führer at the Reichsparteitag.
Having exited Nuremberg's Hauptbahnhof (main railway station), Adolf Hitler, accompanied by Heinrich Himmler (left) inspects the SS guard of honour made up of members of the Leibstandarte-SS Adolf Hitler, Hitler's personal bodyguard regiment. These men were under orders to protect the person of the Führer.

122. The arrival of the Führer at the Reichsparteitag.
Having left the train station the Führer is driven through the streets of Nuremberg to the great delight of the thousands of excited people lining both sides of the street. The crowds are held back by lines of uniformed SS. The SS men control the jubilant public by linking arms to form a human barrier, one man facing the crowd, while the next man faces the street; this is repeated along the entire line. Hitler, standing in his open-top Mercedes 770K salutes the gathered masses, many of whom will have waited hours for this special moment. Daimler-Benz introduced this, their most luxurious car, at the 1930 Paris Motor Show. The 770K had an eight cylinder, 7.7 litre, 150 horsepower engine. An optional supercharger increased this to 200 horsepower. The car had a top speed of about 150km/h. Hitler's midnight blue 770K weighed in at around 5 tonnes due to the 18mm steel armour-plating and the 4cm thick bullet-proof glass. Despite the substantial inbuilt protection, Hitler spent considerable time standing up in these vehicles; this in itself countered the protective elements provided by the vehicle and presented any would-be assassin with a feasible target.

123. The arrival of the Führer.
The Führer continues his journey through the streets of Nuremberg. In the background again we see the Hauptbahnhof. As if to emphasise the point made in the previous caption, this postcard clearly shows the opportunities presented to an assassin by the act of standing up in the vehicle, something Hitler did again and again, particularly when being driven through cities and crowded areas.

124. The Führer greets his Old Guard.
Hitler salutes his old friend and confidant Hermann Göring, one of his earliest supporters, as Göring, then Head of the Luftwaffe, leads the parade as it makes its way through the Adolf-Hitler-Platz.

Behind Göring the ranks of marching men stretch back to the Fleischbrücke. Hermann Göring had played a vital part in the discussions that led to the annexation of Austria earlier that year. In the foreground, bare-headed, stands Deputy Führer, Rudolf Hess.

125. On the Adolf-Hitler-Platz on 11 September 1938.
Adolf Hitler and Hermann Göring shake hands at the 1938 Nazi Party Rally. Between Hitler and Göring stands Rudolf Hess, Deputy Führer. The building in the background is the Rathaus.

126. *Reverse reads:* **Nürnberg – March-past before the Führer.**
Columns of SA (*Sturmabteilung;* Storm Troopers) make their way over the Fleishbrücke towards the Adolf-Hitler-Platz (originally the Hauptmarkt, but renamed the Adolf-Hitler-Platz 1933-45). On reaching the square, located further along the street on the right, Hitler, standing in an open-top Mercedes and surrounded by his entourage would take the salute. These events attracted hundreds of thousands of people.

127. *Reverse reads:* **Nürnberg – City of the Party Congress. Luitpold Arena with Congress Hall and Honour Tribune.**
In the foreground we see one of the grandstands that made up three sides of the Luitpold Arena; in the background the Congress Hall and Tribune. This postcard was posted in Nuremberg on 28 March 1939 to an address in Westphalia. At the time no-one could have guessed that the 1938 Party Congress would be the last of the great Nuremberg Rallies ever to take place. Just five months after this card was posted the world would be on the brink of war.

128. Opening of the Party Congress – Honouring the dead.
SS *Sturmbannführer* (Major) Jakob Grimminger is seen holding the revered *Blutfahne* (Blood Banner) during the opening of the 1938 Party Congress. A who's who of the Nazi leadership stands silently and reverently in the background. From right to left they are; Hermann Göring, Rudolf Hess, Julius Streicher, Adolf Hitler, Heinrich Himmler, Robert Ley, Dr Joseph Goebbels, and Dr Wilhelm Frick.

129. Reichsparteitag.
The massed ranks of the standard-bearers of the SA assemble silently before the Congress Hall in the Luitpold Arena. In the foreground, with backs turned to the camera stand soldiers of the Wehrmacht. This postcard was mailed during the 1938 Nazi Party Rally on 13 September 1938 to an address in Bad Ischl.

130. The great roll-call in the Luitpold Arena: Honouring the heroes.
The Führer, flanked by Himmler (right) and Lutze (left) pay tribute to the fallen while standing solemnly before the huge wreath in front of the Ehrenhalle at the 1938 Nuremberg Rally. They salute those who fell during the First World War, and also the Nazi martyrs of the Munich Beer-Hall *Putsch* (Revolt) of 9 November 1923. Again, the much-revered *Blutfahne* (Blood Banner) carried as always by SS *Sturmbannführer* (Major) Jakob Grimminger makes its appearance for the event. In the background we see the Congress Hall.

131. The great roll-call – the honouring of the dead in the Luitpold Arena.
Another postcard image recording this, the most solemn of Nazi events held in the Luitpold Arena. Having moved position to the other side of the large wreath, the photographer reveals only Hitler and Himmler standing before the *Blutfahne* in this instance.

132. The great roll-call in the Luitpold Arena: Banners and flags marching-up.
The flags and banners of National Socialism come together in the Luitpold Arena, unknowingly for the last time. The arena is filled with the men of the SA and the SS as a military band marches towards the Tribune. Nuremberg's enormous Party Rally Grounds hosts the last of the great National Socialist demonstrations.

133. Rejoicing around the Führer on the Day of the Community.
Hitler climbs the steps to the Congress Hall in the Luitpold Arena. The apparently predominantly female audience, all of whom are seen wearing national costume, push forward as they salute and call out to the smiling Führer. Again the crowds are held back by uniformed members of the SS. During the early years of the regime and even into the first years of the Second World War, Hitler enjoyed unparalleled popularity. Such scenes were commonplace during events where Hitler made public appearances. It can be said that for the most part, Hitler was adored by the vast majority of German women. This was one of the main reasons that Hitler kept his relationship with Eva Braun secret; for he wished to maintain that high level of popularity with German women.

134. Nürnberg, view from the Dutzendteich to the Honour Tribune of the Zeppelin Field.
This unusually peaceful scene shows boating on the Dutzendteich at the *Reichsparteitag-Gelände*. The almost totally deserted Tribune on the Zeppelin Field dominates the background. This postcard bears a commemorative 'Parteitag Großdeutschlands' postmark and was mailed during the 1938 Party Rally in Nuremberg on 10 September 1938.

135. Roll-call of the Reich Labour Service on the Zeppelin Meadow.
In this instance Hitler is observed giving the Nazi salute as members of the RAD parade before him. Standing on the left of the image are; Dr Wilhelm Frick and Rudolf Hess. On the right is Konstantin Hierl, *Reichsarbeitsführer*, head of the *Reichsarbeitsdienst* (RAD; State Labour Service). The RAD was established in July 1934. A law introduced in June 1935 obliged all citizens, both male and female aged 18 to 25 to serve in the RAD. Having served a compulsory period of six months in the RAD, male members then went directly into the Wehrmacht.

During the Second World War the men of the RAD acted as Armed Forces Auxiliaries. Members worked in construction, building defences such as the West Wall along the Atlantic coast. They laid minefields, manned defensive positions, guarded installations and occasionally prisoners. As the tide of war turned against Germany, members of the organization then served in combat units on the Eastern Front. Numerous RAD men fought at the various fronts, while those not suited to front line duty served in anti-aircraft units.

136. Roll-call of the Reich Labour Service on the Zeppelin Meadow.
The men of the RAD parade before the Führer. Again Hitler can be seen standing in his Mercedes limousine. Directly above him we see the *Führerempore* (Führer's rostrum) with Nazi drape attached. But it is the enormous gilded swastika in its wreath that dominates the entire scene. While it has not been posted, this postcard bears a Czechoslovakian stamp on the reverse and a postmark of 30 September 1938. This is a direct reference to the Munich Agreement concluded on the night of 29/30 September 1938. Essentially the Agreement provided the German Army unhindered occupation of the predominantly ethnic German region of the Sudetenland in Czechoslovakia. German troops entered the Sudetenland the following day, 1 October 1938.

137. Uncaptioned.
This image, in fact the last to be acquired prior to publication, shows the massed ranks of the various Nazi organizations, perhaps as many as 50,000 men, formed up in the Luitpold Arena before the Führer. The *Straße des Führers* (the Führer's Way) forms a dividing line running from the podium below the three Nazi banners to the lower right of the photograph.

138. *Reverse reads:* **Nürnberg. Day of the Wehrmacht.**
Hitler, standing on the speaker's rostrum at the Zeppelin Field addresses the assembled members of the new German Wehrmacht (Wehrmacht; the official name for the combined armed forces of the Army, the Navy, and the Air Force during the Third Reich) on the field before him. The term 'Wehrmacht' came into being following a Führer decree on 21 May 1935, thereby replacing the term 'Reichswehr', the term used to describe the 100,000 man army to which Germany was restricted during the period of the Weimar Republic under the terms of the Versailles Treaty. On the field we see members of the German Navy, a number of Panzers (Tanks), cavalry, members of the German Army, and a number of other armoured vehicles. This postcard bears a number of special postmarks on the reverse all commemorating the 1938 Party Congress.

139. Demonstration of the Wehrmacht: Tank attack and defence.
The Zeppelin Field is the venue for these battle-scenes acted out by soldiers of the Wehrmacht. An MG34 machine-gun crew demonstrate the weapon in the face of an attack by Panzers. These 'war games' certainly impressed the onlookers during the 1938 Party Congress. However, neither the audience nor the participants could guess how what they were witnessing here would soon become reality as events that would ultimately lead to the beginning of the Second World War unfolded. The Zeppelin Field was still largely intact at the end of the Second World War. On 22 April 1945 the US Army held a victory parade by the Tribune. At the end of the ceremony the large gilded swastika that crowned the Tribune was blown up.

140. The National Socialist 'Day of the Community'.
Combat Games: The demonstrations on the Zeppelin Field.
Literally thousands of participants line up, in perfect order, to take part in what are described as 'combat games' on the Zeppelin Field before the Führer at the 1938 *Reichsparteitag*. The grandstands around the field are filled to capacity. These 'community events' played an important role in bringing the participants and the audience together in the ideals of National Socialism. But, perhaps more importantly, such events helped to strengthen the bonds that bound the participants and the onlookers to Adolf Hitler. The overall aim of the Nuremberg Rallies was to move, appeal to and impress the masses with the idea of a new, reborn and strong Germany. In presenting Hitler as Germany's saviour, sent by providence, the seeds of the personality cult of Adolf Hitler were sown and would take root.

141. Uncaptioned.
This postcard shows a section of the RAD *(Reichsarbeitsdienst)* camp set up to accommodate members of the organization attending the Party Congress. The very presence of the man in RAD uniform, seen shouldering a spade before the tent in the foreground, identifies this as an RAD camp. This area of the camp is known as the 'Kurpfalz'. The small sign attached to the telegraph pole on the extreme right indicates the way to the 'Lazarett', the military hospital.

Reichsparteitag 1939

The eleventh Nuremberg Rally; *Reichsparteitag des Friedens* (The Rally of Peace), as the theme suggests, intended to demonstrate and celebrate the German will to peace both at home and abroad. Unfortunately, this rally, planned to run from 2 to 11 September 1939 never took place due to the outbreak of the Second World War on 1 September. Amid claim and counterclaim, German forces attacked Poland on Friday, 1 September 1939. Britain declared war on Germany some forty-eight hours later, on 3 September, the rest as they say, is history. Hitler, having cancelled the Party Congress treated Sunday 3 September as if it were a weekday. The Wehrmacht were placed on a semi-emergency basis. All military attachés were ordered to remain in the capital, Berlin, until further notice.

As with the rallies of the preceding years it is reasonable to suppose that the usual postcards produced to advertise and promote the 1939 Nuremberg Rally would have been printed and already in circulation prior to the event. However, to date I have only found the postcard in the so called 'Red Card' series for the 1939 rally. The fact that the rally was cancelled at the last minute means that it is only those promotional postcard images that exist in any case, and there are few of these. For some unknown reason, it appears that these 1939 promotional postcards were never printed in any quantity; this seems very strange. Of course all preparations and planning for that year's *Reichsparteitag* would have been completed. The city of Nuremberg would have been preparing for the annual Party Congress for months and many thousands of people would have already arrived in the city. As already mentioned these were huge events requiring many months of prior planning. The cancellation of the 1939 *Reichsparteitag* must have been a great disappointment to many people, however, the news that the country was at war would have made the cancellation of the event seem insignificant.

Hitler's last peaceful territorial expansion prior to the outbreak of the Second World War was that of the return of the Memelland in March 1939. Situated on the Baltic coast and sandwiched between East Prussia and Lithuania, this former German territory had been under French administration since the end of the First World War. On 9 January 1923 Lithuanian forces entered the Memelland. Amazingly neither the French regional administration nor League of Nations took any serious action against Lithuania's occupation of the region. The area was annexed by Lithuania on 19 January 1939. On 10 March 1939, Joachim von Ribbentrop, Reich Minister for Foreign Affairs, demanded the return of the Memelland to Germany. To increase pressure on the Lithuanians, Hitler personally set out for the port of Memel aboard the pocket battleship 'Deutschland' with threats to invade. Lithuania gave up all claims to the Memelland when a Lithuanian delegation headed by Juozas Urbšys, Lithuanian Minister of Foreign Affairs signed the *Treaty of the Cession of Memel Territory to Germany* in Berlin on 23 March 1939.

Returning to the *Reichsparteitage* of earlier years, it is interesting to note the involvement of one young British aristocrat in these events. Unity Mitford, daughter of David Bertram Ogilvy Freeman-Mitford, 2nd Baron Redesdale, travelled to Germany on a number of occasions with her sister, Diana. Diana Mitford, Unity's elder sister, had an affair with, and subsequently married Sir Oswald Mosley in 1936. Mosley, as leader of the British Union of Fascists that he had founded in 1932 had links with Nazi Germany. The girls' parents held strong right-wing views and were supporters of the BUF (British Union of Fascists).

Unity Mitford, then aged nineteen, on attending the 1933 Nuremberg Rally said of Hitler; *'The first time I saw him I knew there was no one I would rather meet!'* Unity returned to Germany in 1934 where she attended a language school in Munich. She regularly visited the Osteria Bavaria, a restaurant in the city where Hitler ate regularly in the hope of meeting him. Finally, in February 1935 her persistence paid off when she was asked to join Hitler's table. The Führer was quite fascinated by the young British woman with a keen interest in the Nazi movement. Unity made a favourable impression, Hitler once described her as, *'a perfect specimen of Aryan womanhood'*.

Becoming part of Hitler's 'inner circle', the young English aristocrat spent time at the Führer's private residence the Berghof, close to the town of Berchtesgaden. The young woman, an open and ardent Nazi supporter dreamed of some kind of German/British alliance, going so far as to draw up a list of probable supporters amongst the British establishment. It is perfectly reasonable to assume that this list may have played a part in Rudolf Hess's decision to fly to Britain in 1941 in an effort to negotiate peace between the two countries. Unity's access to Hitler and her friendship with him was not well received by all. The fact that she was a cousin of Clementine Hozier, the wife of Winston Churchill must have caused much embarrassment in Britain.

Hitler urged Unity to return to England when war came in 1939. Unity decided to stay, but the feelings of utter betrayal that her country had declared war on Germany drove her to attempt suicide. Unity took a pistol and shot herself in the head. She survived, but the bullet remained lodged in the back of her skull and inoperable. All Unity's medical expenses during this period were paid for by Hitler personally. Unity Mitford finally returned to England in 1940. She died in 1948 having contracted meningitis when the bullet still in her head became infected.

Scheming and Intrigue Revealed

Documents released under the Freedom of Information Act by the British government in August 2008 have, for the first time, revealed the efforts made by amateur diplomat James Lonsdale-Bryans to secure peace between Britain and Germany in 1940. Born in London on 10 May 1893 and educated at Eton, Lonsdale-Bryans, with the approval of then British Foreign Secretary, Lord Halifax, travelled to Italy to meet with Ulrich von Hassell, German Ambassador to Italy in an effort to negotiate a deal. Lonsdale-Bryans proposed that Germany should have a free hand in Europe provided the Germans agreed not to interfere with Britain's colonial empire interests.

While the British Foreign Office was aware of the reasons behind Lonsdale-Bryans' trip to Italy, his efforts later raised concerns that he had 'greatly exceeded his instructions'. Furthermore, the files reveal that the British Secret Service was uncertain as to just how much backing Lonsdale-Bryans had from Lord Halifax, and indeed the extent of the

142. National Party Day Nürnberg.
This postcard was set to be produced to promote and advertise the eleventh, and, as it turned out, never to be held 1939 annual Nazi Party Rally. This is an evocative image; in that all the elements necessary to impart the idea of a rallying call are there. The national eagle dominates the image while the flags of the Nazi Party and the German Kriegsfahne (Battle Flag) fly side by side. The two figures representing the SA and the Army appear almost subject to the will of the state represented by the national eagle high above. This image is the work of Munich artist Hans Friedmann. Friedmann submitted a number of stirring propaganda images for the 1939 Party Rally. Several of these won approval and would have been produced in postcard form had that year's *Reichsparteitag* gone ahead.

This postcard never left the printers. Test runs, using paper that had already been printed on one side only, perhaps paper left over from a cancelled or, a spoiled job, were used to run off what might be termed, set-up, or first proofs to check the quality prior to printing the image on the required more expensive card. The image on the other side of these previously printed sheets was that of a landscape painting. These intended postcards that had been ordered for use during the 1939 Nazi Party Rally never went beyond that first printing stage. For that reason this particular image is quite rare and therefore expensive to buy.

involvement of the British Foreign Secretary in the affair. Lonsdale-Bryans even went so far as to explore the possibility of travelling to Germany to meet with Joachim von Ribbentrop, German Foreign Minister. Had that meeting taken place, the next logical step would have been to arrange a meeting with Hitler himself.

Lonsdale-Bryans' hopes came to nothing when Germany invaded France in 1940 bringing about a rapid decline in any negotiations. Chamberlain resigned as British Prime Minister on 10 May 1940 to be replaced by Winston Churchill. The change in leadership led to Lord Halifax being dispatched to Washington as British ambassador. As for Lonsdale-Bryans, it is said that he was spared jail in an effort to avoid embarrassing the various government departments and members of the British aristocracy in the event of a public trial. It has been said that James Lonsdale-Bryans had not only the support of Lord Halifax, but also that of Lord Brocket, the Duke of Buccleuch, and possibly Chamberlain himself. Is it not amazing how these secrets are only ever made public long after those who might otherwise be held accountable for their actions are long deceased. Such are the privileges bestowed upon those who achieve high public office and are then in a position to pass laws for their own protection.

143. *Reverse reads:* **Festival postcard. Party Congress of Peace. Nürnberg 2-11 September 1939.**
The fifth, and obviously the last postcard to be produced in the so-called 'Red Card' series designed to advertise and promote the 1939 Party Congress. The theme of this rally; *Reichsparteitag des Friedens* (The Rally of Peace) was intended to celebrate Germany's will to peace. Again this postcard was designed by Prof. Richard Klein.

With all preparations complete, the 1939 Party Congress was cancelled due to the outbreak of the Second World War on 1 September 1939, the day prior to the opening of the planned Annual Party Congress on 2 September. As to the 'Red Card' series, it is interesting to note that the circular designs seen on the postcards were produced as metal badges. These were known as 'Day Badges' and could be purchased by anyone attending the rallies.

GESAMTPLAN:
1. Luitpoldhalle
2. Luitpoldarena
3. Turm d. Ehrentribüne in der Luitpoldarena
4. Gefallenendenkmal
5. Kongreßbau
6. Bau für die Kulturtagungen
7. Ausstellungsbau
8. Zeppelinfeld
9. Tribünenbau des Zeppelinfeld
10. Altes Stadion
11. Das Deutsche Stadion
12. Märzfeld

Reichsparteitag-Gelände in Nürnberg

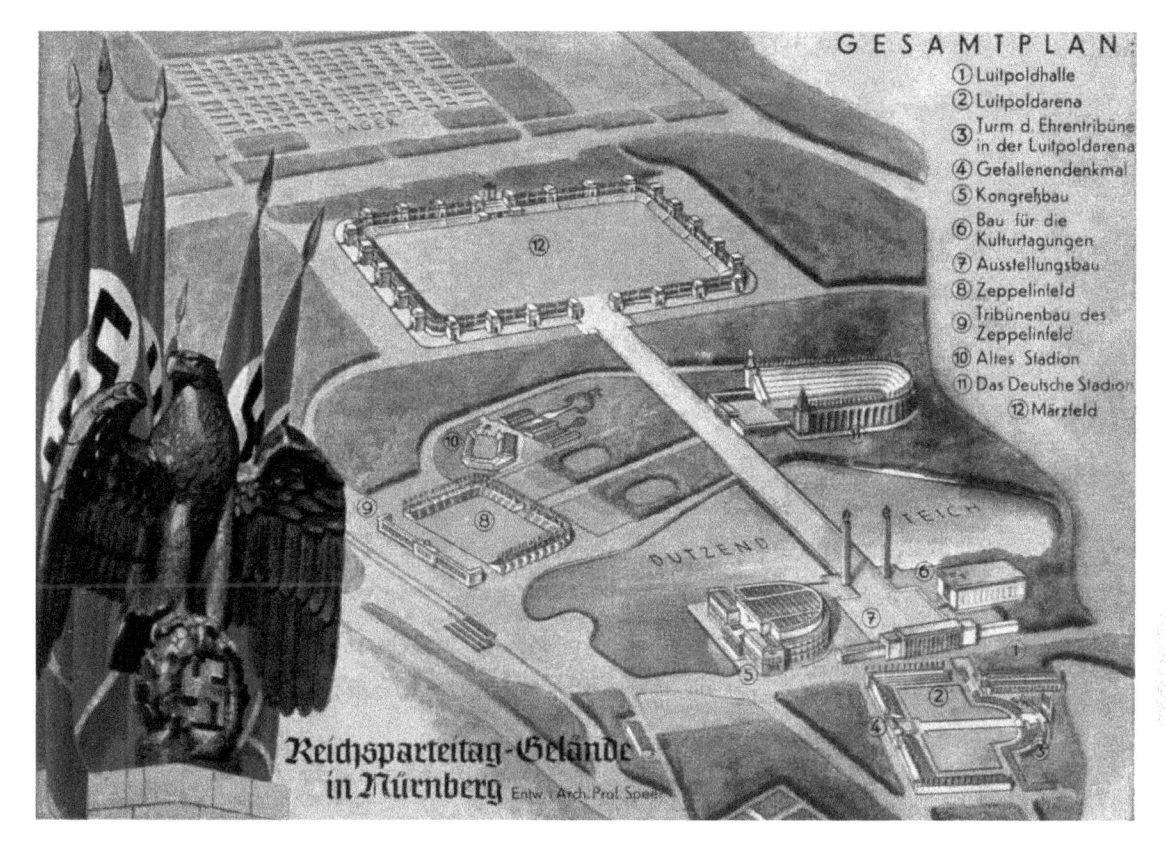

144. National Party Day Rally Grounds in Nürnberg.
This impression of the *Gesamtplan* (Total Plan) was drawn by Professor Albert Speer. It reveals the truly ambitious plans the Nazi Party had for the area. Albert Speer was the architect responsible for the vast majority of buildings constructed at the Rally Grounds, whether actually completed or those still in the planning stage. The image gives a good overall view of the Rally Grounds and the locations of the various structures in relation to each other. The area at the top left of the image marked 'LAGER', is where the huge SA camp was sited (see postcard number 67). This 'LAGER' area is where the campsites for the various organizations attending *Reichsparteitag* were accommodated. These included sections set aside for the Hitler Youth, the SA, the NSKK, the SS, the Wehrmacht and the RAD.

The Rally Grounds would cover an area of some 11 square kilometres, what remains of them today still occupies 4 square kilometres. Part of the site earmarked for the development of the Rally Grounds was taken up by Nuremberg's zoo. This resulted in the entire zoo being relocated to the Schmausenbuck area east of the city in 1939. Again this postcard, like number 141, never went further than the proofing stage on the printing machine. It too was printed on previously used paper. The reverse side of this postcard image shows a small part of an unidentified landscape painting together with the signature of Yugoslavian artist, Hans Bogojevic (1894-1967).

The Nazi Leaders

The following is a brief history of the main Nazi leaders, those individuals who appear and are mentioned in the preceding pages. The majority of these men were early supporters of Adolf Hitler. Their assistance and loyalty to the Führer would lead to important positions in the Nazi government following the coming to power in January 1933.

Martin Bormann

145. Reichsleiter (Reich Leader) Martin Bormann.
Martin Bormann, initially Chief of Staff to Deputy Führer, Rudolf Hess. Bormann was appointed *Reichsleiter* (Reich Leader) in 1933 and finally Secretary to the Führer on 12 April 1943.

This photograph shows Hitler addressing a number of Nazi officials. Second from the left is Rudolf Hess, Deputy Führer, third from the left is Dr Wilhelm Frick, Reich Minister of the Interior, third from the right and most attentive is Martin Bormann. Bormann's demeanour is one of near total subservience.

Martin Ludwig Bormann was born in Halberstadt, Lower Saxony, on 17 June 1900. His father, Theodore (1862-1903) a former sergeant in a cavalry regiment and later postal worker died when Martin was barely four years old. Martin Bormann was drafted towards the end of the First World War and served as a gunner with Field Artillery Regiment 55; he saw little, if any action. After the First World War Bormann worked as an inspector in agriculture and eventually joined the *Freikorps* (Free Corps).

The *Freikorps* were paramilitary units made up of former army officers, demobilized soldiers, adventurers, nationalists, and the unemployed. These right-wing groups blamed the Social Democrats and the Jews for Germany's ills. Their main objective was to eliminate anyone whom they believed might be considered a 'traitor to the Fatherland'. The German Army, also believing in the 'stab in the back' theory secretly supported the *Freikorps.*

Martin Bormann, as a member of the Rossback Freikorps unit operating in Mecklenburg, was implicated in the murder of one Walther Kadow. Kadow had allegedly betrayed a *Freikorps* officer, Albert Leo Schlageter. Tried on charges of espionage and sabotage, Schlageter had been executed by the French near Düsseldorf on 26 May 1923. Bormann, for his part, was subsequently found guilty of complicity in the murder of Kadow and served one year in prison in Leipzig. Following his release, Bormann came into contact with the NSDAP and began working in the Party's press section in Thuringia. In 1928 Bormann was promoted to work for the Chief of Staff of the SA. Bormann was a good organizer and soon acquired an excellent understanding of the workings of the Party.

In 1929 Martin Bormann married Gerda Bach, the daughter of the President of the Party Court. The fact that Adolf Hitler acted as a witness at the ceremony confirms Bormann's ascendancy as a rising star in the Party hierarchy. The Nazi Party achieved power in Germany in January 1933 and soon after Martin Bormann was promoted to the position of Chief of Staff to Deputy Führer, Rudolf Hess. Bormann, the intriguer, the manipulator, was slowly but steadily working his way into Hitler's inner circle. While Bormann had a number of extra marital affairs, his wife Gerda, knowing of his infidelities, complained little. The film star Manja Behrend was Bormann's mistress for a considerable time. On the subject of Manja Behrend, Gerda Bormann wrote; *'See to it that one year she has a child and the next year I have a child, so that you will always have a wife who is serviceable.'* Nonetheless, it is said that Bormann remained in love with Gerda throughout. She bore him ten children. Gerda Bormann died of cancer in March 1946; she is buried in Merano, Italy. All ten Bormann children survived the Second World War.

It was Bormann who oversaw the acquisition of land and property on the Obersalzberg above Berchtesgaden when it was decided to create the *Führersperrgebiet* (Restricted Area of the Führer). This led to the creation of a fenced in area of approximately 800 hectares (2,000 acres). Ambitious, and ruthless in his methods, Martin Bormann was hated by the local population around Berchtesgaden. Indeed even his own colleagues, those in the higher echelons of the Nazi Party, neither liked nor trusted him. Nonetheless, he was possessed of enormous energy and could survive on a mere three or four hours sleep a night. Indeed it was Bormann who conceived the idea of building the Kehlsteinhaus (Eagle's Nest) as a gift from the Party to Hitler on the occasion of his 50th birthday. Bormann's moment came with the flight of Rudolf Hess to Britain on 10 May 1941. While it is generally accepted that Hitler was fully aware of Hess's plans, it had been agreed that if Hess were unsuccessful in his attempt to negotiate peace with Britain, the Deputy Führer had acted alone.

Martin Bormann was promoted head of the newly created *Parteikanzlei* (Party Chancellery) that same day. Bormann became so powerful that he eventually controlled access to Hitler. Even high-ranking officers could not gain an audience with Hitler without first going through Bormann. Martin Bormann did everything possible to secure his position within Hitler's inner circle. In the end, even Hitler came to realize that he had come to rely too much on Bormann. In the last days in Berlin in 1945, Hitler confided to Eva Braun that he had seen through Bormann, and, had things been different, he would have replaced Bormann.

It is said that Bormann was so confident of his position that he would send out 'Führer Orders', orders in the name of the Führer, in the knowledge that no-one would be prepared to question their origin. Adolf Hitler married Eva Braun in the bunker of the Berlin Reich's Chancellery on 29 April 1945. This time Bormann acted as witness for Hitler. The Führer committed suicide the next day, Monday 30 April 1945, at about 3.30 in the afternoon. Soon after, Bormann made his bid for freedom. Travelling in civilian clothes with a small group Bormann left the bunker. For many years it was believed that Bormann had escaped. Indeed there were numerous reported sightings of Bormann in countries in South America during the years after the Second World War. However, in 1972 groundwork close to the Lehrter station in Berlin uncovered two skeletons. One of these was quite quickly identified as that of Dr Ludwig Stumpfegger, one of Hitler's physicians. As for the other, it took almost two years searching dental records before these remains were finally identified as those of Martin Bormann. Shards of glass found in Bormann's jaw led to the conclusion that he had committed suicide using a cyanide capsule. Bormann's decision to attempt to escape an encircled Berlin was unlikely to succeed, but the decision to end his life was probably one forced upon him as he observed large numbers of advancing Soviet troops moving through the city. This final decision was based on a determination not to be taken alive.

Joseph Goebbels

Dr Paul Joseph Goebbels was born in the small town of Rheydt in the Rhineland on 29 October 1897. Goebbels had suffered polio as a child; this left him with a crippled left foot and weakened leg for the rest of his life. An extremely bright boy, Goebbels compensated for his physical weakness by indulging an almost insatiable appetite for reading. It was in Munich in 1922 that Joseph Goebbels heard Adolf Hitler speak for the first time. So impressed was Goebbels that he immediately joined the Nazi Party. This was the beginning of a journey that would see Goebbels become a dedicated follower of Hitler, almost without exception, for the remainder of his life.

Like Hitler, Goebbels was a very gifted speaker. The unexpected success of the Communists in Berlin through 1926 prompted Hitler to send Goebbels to the capital to re-organize the Party there and win the city back from the Communists. There had been much political infighting amongst the Party leadership in the capital. On his arrival in Berlin Goebbels encountered abject apathy, generated for the most part by a conflict-ridden leadership and a lack of organization. Nonetheless within twelve months Goebbels had broken the supremacy of the Strasser brothers in northern Germany and

146. Reich's Minister Dr Goebbels.
Dr Paul Joseph Goebbels, Hitler's Minister for Public Enlightenment and Propaganda.

had turned the Party's fortunes around. As *Gauleiter* (District Leader), Goebbels' gifts for inflammatory speechmaking and innovative campaigning methods proved a successful combination. Notwithstanding the winning of numerous street battles that regularly took place between the SA and the Communists.

In July 1927 Goebbels established *Der Angriff* (The Attack), the Berlin Party's weekly newspaper which he edited. The aim of *Der Angriff* was to discredit and to attack the political opponents of the Nazi Party in the capital. Later, following the announcement of the *Nürnberger Gesetze* (Nuremberg Laws) at the 1935 Party Rally, Goebbels used *Der Angriff* to urge all Party members to take violent action against the Jews. This was done for two reasons; firstly, it was hoped that in stirring up further hatred of the Jews that this would turn the attention of a now grumbling public and faltering Party support towards a 'common enemy'. Secondly, it was intended to increase pressure on the Jews to consider leaving Germany.

Joseph Goebbels was undoubtedly a brilliant propagandist; as time passed he would be instrumental in creating the idea of the Hitler myth, presenting the Führer as Germany's messiah. As a reward for winning Berlin back for the Party, Hitler appointed Goebbels head of propaganda. The 'little doctor' set about introducing dramatic effects to the Nazi rallies and meetings. Geobbels played an important role in the campaigns that eventually led to the Nazis achieving power in Germany in 1933. In recognition of his efforts, Hitler appointed him; Minister for Public Enlightenment and Propaganda. Goebbels then poured his considerable energy into gaining control over the press and radio. His next move was to bring cinema, publishing, and the theatre under his control. Goebbels' power over what was seen, heard, and thought, was considerable.

Joseph Goebbels married Magda Quandt, a divorcee with a ten year son Harald, on 19 December 1931. Johanna Maria Magdalena 'Magda' Quandt, nee Behrend, was born in Berlin on 11 November 1901. On 4 January 1921 she married Günther Quandt, a wealthy German industrialist twice her age. Their only son Harald was born on 1 November 1921. The couple divorced in 1929. Magda joined the NSDAP in September 1930. She came into contact with Joseph Goebbels in the course of her work for the Party. Goebbels was completely taken with the attractive young blond and pursued her relentlessly. Magda Goebbels tolerated her husband's numerous affairs. But when her husband took up with the Czech actress, Lida Baarova, Magda had had enough. She spoke to Hitler and threatened to divorce her husband. The Führer intervened, and Goebbels ended his affair with Baarova. Lida Baarova died in Salzburg, Austria, on 27 October 2000 aged 86.

Constantly striving to ensure that the public were continuously subjected to an endless diet of propaganda, in 1933 the Nazis introduced the *'Volksempfänger'* (People's Radio). The Rundfunkgerät model VE 301 W, was an affordable radio that was produced in large numbers with the idea that no-one should be beyond the reach of the Führer's spoken word or the Party's message. Again, the Party introduced the latest technological advances, including television. Television sets were placed in community centres in the knowledge that this latest media innovation would attract mass public attention. Indeed, the Nazis introduced the world's first public service broadcasts.

Goebbels was not in favour of war, but when war came, he did everything in his power to inspire the people. He was one of but a few of the Nazi leaders who continually visited areas devastated by Allied bombing as the Second World War progressed to its inevitable conclusion. In the final days Joseph Goebbels, his wife Magda and their six children took refuge in the bunker beneath the Reich's Chancellery in Berlin. Following the suicide of Adolf and Eva Hitler on 30 April 1945, Goebbels concluded that he had no wish to continue living in a Germany without his Führer. Having considered what fate might lie in store for their children if they fell into Russian hands, Joseph and Magda Goebbels took the following drastic action. Magda, accompanied by one of Hitler's physicians still in the bunker attended the six children. While Magda explained to the children that they were to be given injections for health reasons, the doctor proceeded to administer injections of morphine to each child in turn. A little later, while the children were asleep, Magda returned alone. Then, working her way around the room, she carefully placed a single cyanide capsule into the mouth of each child taking care to ensure that each capsule was broken.

That done, she and her husband exited the bunker. Joseph and Magda Goebbels ended their lives in the Reich's Chancellery garden close to the bunker entrance, not far from where the remains of Adolf and Eva Hitler lay. Magda took cyanide while Joseph Goebbels shot himself. Their bodies were then set alight with the remaining fuel that had been collected for the purposes of burning the bodies of Hitler and his wife the previous day. The Russians discovered the remains on taking the Reich's Chancellery soon after.

Hermann Göring

Hermann Wilhelm Göring was born in Rosenheim east of Munich on 12 January 1893. When he was only twelve years old Hermann Göring went off to the military academy at Karlsruhe. He left Karlsruhe aged sixteen with good results. Göring then attended the officer cadet training college at Lichterfelde near Berlin. On successful completion of his exams, Göring left Lichterfelde, aged nineteen, to join the 112th Prince Wilhelm Regiment. Hermann Göring was twenty years old when the First World War began. Göring's greatest wish was to join his friend, Bruno Loerzer in the Imperial Air Corps. He submitted an application, and following certain irregularities and close to the mark methods, his wish was granted. Hermann Göring quickly earned a reputation as a brave and competent pilot.

In 1917 he was appointed commander of a new squadron, *Jagdstaffel* 27, based in Flanders. A *Jagdstaffel* is a formation consisting of between nine and twelve aircraft. Göring went on to win the *Pour le Mérite,* Germany's highest military honour. The *Pour le Mérite* was normally awarded to those who had shot down twenty-five enemy aircraft. However with only fifteen victories to his credit at the time, Hermann Göring received the prestigious award for his leadership qualities and professionalism. Göring was given command of the famous 'Richthofen Squadron' following the untimely death of its commander, Manfred Albrecht Freiherr von Richthofen (1882-1918) better known as the 'Red Baron'. Hermann Göring ended the First World War with twenty victories.

After the war Göring spent considerable time travelling in Denmark and Sweden demonstrating Fokker aircraft. It was while working in Sweden that Göring met his first wife Karin von Kantzow. The fact that this lady was already married and had a son made no difference to Göring. Sadly, Karin died of tuberculosis on 17 October 1931. Göring

147. The Reich's Marshal.
Hermann Wilhelm Göring, Head of the German Luftwaffe.

was devastated at the loss of his wife. It was in 1922 while in Munich that Hermann Göring encountered Adolf Hitler for the first time. Soon after this encounter, Göring joined the NSDAP. Göring was well connected; he knew influential people and could arrange introductions that would prove beneficial to the Party. On taking part in the Munich Beer-Hall *Putsch* on 9 November 1923, Göring was badly wounded. He received treatment in Austria, unfortunately the amounts of morphine he received during his recovery led to an addiction from which he would never fully recover. Additionally the treatment affected his glands which in turn led to an increase in body weight.

Göring was elected to the Reichstag in 1928. Following Nazi electoral success during the 1932 elections Hermann Göring became President of the Reichstag. When the Nazis came to power in 1933, Göring received a number of important appointments. He became; Reich Minister without Portfolio, Reich Commissioner for Air, Prussian Minister President, and Prussian Minister of the Interior. As Reich Commissioner for Air, Göring initiated plans to build a strong air force for Germany. This was carried out in secrecy as the terms of the Versailles Treaty denied Germany the right to an air force. Nonetheless, by the time Hitler announced the existence of the German *Luftwaffe* to the world in March 1935; the Allied powers stood by and barely reacted.

On 10 April 1935 Hermann Göring married the actress Emmy Sonnemann. Adolf Hitler acted as best man. The much publicized wedding was a high point in the Nazi calendar at the time. The couple's only child Edda, was born on 2 June 1938. Göring adored the little girl. Both mother and daughter survived the Second World War. Edda and her mother spent four years in an Allied prison camp after the war. Emmy Göring died in Munich on 8 June 1973.

Hermann Göring rightly believed that Germany could not win a protracted war. When the Second World War began in September 1939, Göring tried to impress upon Hitler the importance of defeating England prior to any thoughts of invading the Soviet Union. Hitler, however, held to the belief that peace could and would be negotiated with Britain, eventually. Göring was right; he knew that the *Luftwaffe* was not strong enough to fight a war on two fronts. With the fall of France in June 1940, Hermann Göring was promoted Field Marshal. As the war situation deteriorated, and with defeat staring them in the face, Hitler and a number of the Nazi hierarchy took refuge in Berlin. The Allies had received information to suggest that Hitler might leave Berlin on 20 April 1945 and make his way to the Obersalzberg above Berchtesgaden. An aircraft did leave Berlin on 20 April and fly down to Bavaria, but it was Hermann Göring, not Adolf Hitler who made his way to the Obersalzberg. On 23 April, Göring sent a telegram to Hitler in Berlin. The telegram proposed the following; that he, Göring, given that he enjoyed a greater level of freedom of movement than Hitler in Berlin, should assume leadership of the Reich. Furthermore, Göring suggested the idea of his making efforts to contact the Western Allies to explore the possibilities of arriving at some form of a negotiated surrender.

Hitler's initial reaction was one of relative calm. However, Göring's arch-enemy Bormann lost no time in deliberately twisting and misrepresenting the entire content of the telegram to a point where Hitler believed that Göring had betrayed him. Hitler immediately ordered Göring's house arrest; and so Hermann Göring was held under guard in his own home on the Obersalzberg. Two days later, on 25 April an Allied air raid consisting of over 300 Lancaster and Mosquito bombers attacked the Obersalzberg. Most of the buildings on the mountain, including Hitler's Berghof, suffered considerable damage. Göring and his guards sat out the air raid in the bunker beneath the Göring home. When the raid was over, Göring and his guards re-emerged to an unrecognizable landscape. The guards, following a short private discussion, decided there was little point in remaining on scene and promptly left.

Hermann Göring was picked up on 9 May 1945 by US forces near Salzburg in Austria. He subsequently stood trial alongside the remaining Nazi leaders at Nürnberg. Göring was the one man who stood out amongst the defendants during the trials. He was found guilty and sentenced to death by hanging. Hermann Göring's request that, as a military man he should be shot by firing-squad was denied. Göring, like so many other Nazi leaders, denied the hangman. He was found dying in his cell on 15 October 1946, just a matter of hours before the sentence was due to be carried out. Only in recent years has it come to light as to how Hermann Göring acquired the cyanide capsule with which he killed himself. The young GI who was standing guard before the door to Göring's cell, had Göring's fountain pen in his possession. Göring had pleaded for the pen to write some final letters. Göring went so far as to offer a trade; his wristwatch for the pen. Eventually the trade took place; Göring got his fountain pen, and the cyanide capsule hidden inside it.

Rudolf Hess

Walter Richard Rudolf Hess was born in Alexandria, Egypt on 26 April 1894. Rudolf was the eldest son of Fritz Hess, a successful German businessman who had emigrated to Egypt. When in 1908 his father bought property in Bavaria, Rudolf Hess returned to Germany to continue his studies at a school in Godesberg-am-Rhein. Coming as he did from an upper middle class family background Hess was well educated. Rudolf Hess served as a lieutenant with the 16th Bavarian Reserve Infantry Regiment during the First World War. He was wounded three times; the last time seriously. On his release from hospital Hess joined the Imperial Air Corps. He had just completed his pilot training when the First World War came to an end. Hess was demobilized in December 1918.

His right-wing leanings led Hess to join the *Freikorps* in 1919. In 1920 Hess entered the university in Munich to study economics, history, and geopolitics – the study of the influence upon the politics of a country through its geographical position. Hess maintained an interest in politics over many years. It was through a chance encounter in 1920 that Hess heard Hitler speak for the first time. The young Hess was so impressed that he joined the fledgling NSDAP soon after. Rudolf Hess quickly became a constant companion of Adolf Hitler. Hess often fought alongside the SA in the numerous street battles against the Communists.

Hess marched beside Hitler on the morning of 9 November 1923 during the Beer-Hall *Putsch*. Somehow in the aftermath of the debacle Hess managed to escape across the border into Austria. Following the trials held in Munich in 1924 and Hitler's resulting prison sentence, Hess returned, and was himself imprisoned for his part in the revolt. Hess joined Hitler in Landsberg Prison where most of his time was occupied acting as

148. Rudolf Hess. Deputy Führer.
Rudolf Hess photographed wearing SS uniform. Hess held the honorary rank of *Obergruppenführer* (Lieutenant-General) in the SS.

secretary to Hitler; he was of great help to Hitler during the writing of *Mein Kampf*. The two men developed a close bond during the period of their incarceration.

Hess married Ilse Pröhl, the daughter of a wealthy physician on 20 December 1927. The couple had one child, a son, Wolf-Rüdiger born on 18 December 1937. Ilse Hess died in Lilienthal on 7 September 1995. Rudolf Hess played an important part in the electoral campaign that would eventually see Hitler appointed Chancellor on 30 January 1933. His reward was to be appointed Deputy Führer on 21 April 1933. Hess spent considerable time on the Obersalzberg, and at Hitler's country home, the Berghof. Those amongst the Party hierarchy, that is those who did not have their own homes on the Obersalzberg, people like Hess and Goebbels, were accommodated in the Party guesthouse, Villa Bechstein, just below the Berghof. Hitler and Hess spent many hours together discussing politics and other subjects during the long periods spent on the Obersalzberg.

The flight of Hess to Scotland on 10 May 1941 remains something of a mystery to this day. The idea that Hitler knew nothing of Hess's planned flight is most unlikely. The two men spent four hours in private conversation just days prior to the Deputy Führer's departure. Hess had planned to meet with the Duke of Hamilton, whom he already knew. Suffice to say that at that stage of the conflict there were still a number of highly placed individuals in Britain, amongst them members of the then British government, who were still disposed to a negotiated settlement with Germany. Hess took off from Augsburg in a Messerschmitt Bf 110 fitted with auxiliary fuel-tanks on 10 May 1941. Hess failed in his mission. Had he been successful, Germany would probably have won the Second World War by not having to fight a war on two fronts, against Britain and her allies in the west, and the Soviet Union in the east. Hess was held at various locations around Britain until the Second World War ended, he was then brought back to Germany to stand trial alongside the other surviving Nazi leaders.

Rudolf Hess was found guilty and sentenced to life imprisonment. So it was, that when all other Nazi leaders had either been executed, or had been released having served jail sentences, that Rudolf Hess, prisoner number 7, was the last man to be held in Spandau Prison in Berlin. Thus a prison of 600 cells was home to just one man, a very expensive undertaking. Eventually, Britain, France and the United States would agree that Hess might be released on humanitarian grounds. The Russians however, would never agree, they would continually veto such a move. Much controversy and speculation surrounds the mysterious death of Rudolf Hess. He was found hanged in a summer house in the grounds of Spandau Prison on 17 August 1987. At the time of his death Hess was almost 93 years old and in poor health. He walked with the aid of a stick and could not rise from a chair unaided. Nonetheless, despite these infirmities, Rudolf Hess still managed to hang himself with a piece of electric wire.

The affidavit of Abdallah Melaouhi, the civilian male nurse who had attended Rudolf Hess during the last five years of his life makes most interesting reading. What information did Hess have that might embarrass or even destroy the reputations of so many people that it would for ever prevent his release. Why have so many successive governments refused to release the paperwork surrounding his capture and subsequent interrogation. Many unanswered questions surround the imprisonment and death of the former Deputy Führer. Rudolf Hess is buried in Wunsiedel in northeast Bavaria.

Heinrich Himmler

Heinrich Luitpold Himmler was born in Munich on 7 October 1900. His father, Joseph, was a secondary school teacher. Heinrich had two brothers, Gebhard, born on 29 July 1898 and Ernst, born on 23 December 1905. As a student Himmler did well at school. Towards the end of 1917 he began officer training with the 11th Bavarian Infantry Regiment. Himmler never managed to see action during the First World War; this would remain a source of irritation to him for the rest of his life. Having left the army Heinrich Himmler became a student of agriculture at the Munich Technische Hochschule in 1919. In 1920 Himmler met Captain Ernst Röhm. Röhm recruited Himmler to the NSDAP and introduced him to Adolf Hitler. Having successfully completed his studies Himmler found employment as an agriculturist in Schlessheim. Himmler took part in the unsuccessful Beer-Hall *Putsch* on 9 November 1923. Amazingly, Himmler somehow managed to avoid both injury and arrest. In July 1928 Himmler married Margarete Boden, almost eight years his senior. The rather unhappy marriage produced one child, a daughter, Gudrun, born on 8 August 1929, whom Himmler adored. The couple separated soon after the birth of their child. Gudrun Himmler was presented as the perfect German child and spoiled

149. The Reichsführer-SS visiting SS Panzer-Grenadier-Regiment 'Der Führer'.
Heinrich Luitpold Himmler, Head of the SS, the police, and the Gestapo.
This postcard shows Himmler (centre) in discussion with *Brigadeführer* (Major-General) Dr Otto Wachter and *Brigadeführer* Friedrich Freitag while visiting SS Panzer-Grenadier-Regiment 'Der Führer'.

by her adoring father. Somewhat strange is the fact that Gudrun occasionally accompanied her father when he visited the concentration camps.

Himmler paid great attention to detail and was very methodical in his approach to all tasks. In January 1929 Hitler appointed Himmler head of a recently formed small group existing within the much larger SA, the SS. Himmler brought his considerable organizational skills into play and set about building up the SS and introducing strict recruitment criteria. Hitler, for his part, took little interest initially, but gave his approval to Himmler's plans. By 1933 the SS had grown to a force of about 50,000 men. In 1940 Himmler began an affair with his secretary, Hedwig Potthast; she bore him two children, a son Helge, born in 1942, and a daughter Nanette, born in 1944.

During the Second World War the Waffen-SS (Military SS) fought on every front. The men of the Waffen-SS quickly earned a reputation for being very tough soldiers. Himmler had created an elite force, one to be feared on the battlefield. In the end the Waffen-SS consisted of thirty-eight divisions, almost one million men. In April 1934 Himmler was given control of the *Geheime Staatspolizei* (Gestapo; Secret State Police). In June 1936 he became Chief of German Police with the title *Reichsführer-SS.* In 1943 he replaced Wilhelm Frick as Reich Minister of the Interior. Himmler had far reaching powers. He oversaw the setting up and running of the first concentration camps prior to the outbreak of the Second World War with his usual efficiency and meticulous attention to detail.

By 1944 Himmler realized that Germany could no longer win the war. This realization eventually led him to thoughts of self-preservation. In February 1945 Himmler had a meeting with Count Folke Bernadotte, a representative of the Swedish Red Cross. The meeting took place to discuss the possible release of Danish and Norwegian prisoners held in the concentration camp system. This was the first stage in Himmler's bid to gain favour with the Allies. Later, and as the military situation deteriorated, his efforts became more frantic. He went so far as to ask Folke Bernadotte to attempt to arrange a meeting with Eisenhower. His efforts came to nothing. Hitler, on learning of Himmler's actions, commented that this was the worst act treachery he had ever known.

With the Führer dead and the war over, Himmler attempted to evade capture. Shaving off his moustache and wearing an eye-patch he further attempted to disguise himself by wearing a tattered sergeant's uniform. Himmler and his travelling companions were picked up near Bremervörde west of Hamburg on 21 May 1945. Himmler's downfall was the fact that he presented brand new identification papers to British troops manning a checkpoint at a time when hardly anyone could produce any papers at all, let alone newly issued and complete. He was subsequently arrested and brought to Lüneburg for questioning. Two days later on 23 May 1945, having admitted his identity and while being medically examined, Heinrich Himmler bit down hard on a cyanide capsule hidden in his mouth and died on the spot. His body was buried in an unmarked grave on Lüneburg Heath on 26 May 1945.

Adolf Hitler

Adolf Hitler was born in the small Austrian town of Braunau-am-Inn on 20 April 1889. It was there that his father, Alois, worked as an Inspector of Customs on the Austrian/German border. Alois Hitler, (1837-1903) despite rather humble beginnings, had done well to achieve a position of which he was justly proud. A strict disciplinarian, Alois administered physical punishment to his rebellious son Adolf on an almost daily basis. Hitler's mother, Klara, (1860-1907) on the other hand always tried to protect her son. Where his father failed to gain obedience through toughness and beatings, Hitler's mother proved the more successful with her gentle ways, appeals, and persuasion. Needless to say, Adolf Hitler adored his mother. On retiring from the Customs Service, Alois Hitler moved the family to Leonding just outside Linz. It was there on the morning

150. Uncaptioned.
Adolf Hitler, German Führer and head of the NSDAP.

of 3 January 1903 while out for his morning walk that Hitler's father suddenly felt unwell. He made his way into his local inn, Gasthaus Stiefler, were he died of a pleural haemorrhage. Klara Hitler moved the family to Urfahr, a suburb of Linz soon after her husband's death.

Since he had been a boy Adolf Hitler had dreamed of being an artist; a subject upon which he and his father continually disagreed. With his father now dead, Hitler moved to Vienna in the hope of pursuing that dream. He sat the entrance exam to the Academy of Fine Arts in Vienna in October 1907, but was rejected on the grounds that it was felt his work lacked imagination. This was a great blow to the would-be artist, nonetheless Hitler remained in Vienna. Towards the end of November that year Hitler received word that his mother was unwell and that he should return home. Hitler returned to Linz to find that his mother was in fact dying of breast cancer. Taking charge, Adolf Hitler tenderly nursed his mother through her final weeks; she died on 21 December 1907. Hitler was emotionally devastated.

Adolf Hitler returned to Vienna soon after his mother's passing. He had a small allowance, and this combined with what money he earned from selling small, postcard sized drawings and watercolours that he produced of the better known buildings around the city provided enough to rent a room and to feed himself. Towards the end of 1908 Hitler returned to the Academy of Fine Arts with the intention of sitting the entrance exam a second time. Unfortunately for him, some of those who had judged the work the previous year recognized him and he was not allowed to sit the exam. While Hitler had continually sent part of his own small allowance to help his younger sister Paula, his own financial situation got steadily worse. In the end he could no longer afford the room and he was forced to live on the streets. It was through this situation that Hitler first came into contact with those possessed of extreme political views while living in the city's homeless men's hostels.

Turning his back on Vienna, Adolf Hitler left the city in 1913 and made his way to Munich. It has been said that Hitler made this move to avoid the draft. Apparently he had received notification from the Austrian authorities that he was required to do military service. However, in February 1914 Hitler presented himself in Salzburg, Austria, for medical examination. His lifestyle prior to this point had been one of living rough and irregular eating habits for the most part with the result that he was considered unfit for military service. The medical report concluded with the line; 'too weak to bear arms'. Hitler returned to Munich.

At the outbreak of the First World War in August 1914, Hitler immediately volunteered. However, as an Austrian, he had to seek permission to be allowed to serve in the German Army. To his great delight, this was granted. Adolf Hitler served through the entire period of the First World War with the 16th Bavarian Reserve Infantry Regiment (List Regiment). Hitler proved a brave and able soldier. During four years he took part in no less than forty-seven battles, often in the middle of the fighting. He was wounded in the leg in October 1917 and the victim of a gas attack in late 1918. Adolf Hitler would win the Iron Cross, both First and Second Class during the conflict. The gas attack left Hitler temporarily blinded. It was while he was recovering from these injuries in hospital at Pasewalk that the First World War came to and end. Adolf Hitler, like many of his comrades, felt that the German Army, while it had not been defeated on the battlefield, had been dealt a stab in the back by the weak politicians at home.

Hitler was finally released from hospital but he remained in military service. In 1919 he underwent training as a 'political officer'. Having completed his training, Hitler's job was to ensure that the troops were not influenced by those advocating socialist, pacifist, and even democratic ideas. Again in 1919 the head of the political section of the army gave Hitler a specific task. He was instructed to attend, in civilian clothes, the meetings of both left and right wing political groups around the city of Munich. His job was to go along to these meetings, listen to what was being said and then report his findings to his superiors. In this way it was hoped to learn what was happening at a grass roots level on the then turbulent political scene.

It was while doing this work that Adolf Hitler first came in contact with a particular small right-wing group, the *Deutsche Arbeiterpartei* (German Workers' Party) in September 1919. Going along to the meetings Hitler discovered that the views of the party were actually very similar to his own views. Hitler joined the German Workers' Party as member number 55. It was then that Hitler discovered that he could hold an audience through the power of his oratory. He was soon addressing the meetings of the German Workers' Party on a regular basis and encouraging new membership. Hitler finally left the army in April 1920.

By July 1921 Adolf Hitler had won the internal battle for control of the party, now renamed the *Nationalsozialistische Deutsche Arbeiterpartei* (NSDAP; National Socialist German Workers' Party). On 9 November 1923 the Nazis attempted to seize power in Bavaria when they carried out the Munich Beer-Hall *Putsch* (Revolt). The attempt failed, and Hitler subsequently stood trial on a charge of treason. If convicted, and given the maximum penalty under the law, Hitler was in fact facing a death penalty. The trails began on 28 February 1924. Of the accused, Adolf Hitler would dominate the proceedings. Thanks to the intervention of powerful friends in the Justice Ministry, and while highly irregular, Hitler was permitted to cross-examine witnesses. Additionally, he was allowed to make what amounted to speeches and proclamations promoting the party's ideals during the trials. Again, thanks to the intervention of these same powerful friends and a judge who was not unsympathetic towards the Nazis, Hitler was sentenced to five years imprisonment on 1 April 1924. This, in fact, was the minimum sentence that could be handed down to a person convicted of treason.

The trials attracted great media attention. The press reported the trials throughout Germany and beyond on a daily basis. Hitler seized upon the interest of the press, here was his opportunity, and he made the most of it. By the end of the proceedings Hitler had emerged as both victim and patriot. He and his party had achieved a level of publicity they could otherwise never have dreamed of. The *Putsch* had not been a failure after all. It was around this time that Adolf Hitler decided that all further attempts to achieve power would be by legal means. In the meantime, he was dispatched to the prison fortress at Landsberg-am-Lech to serve his sentence. On his arrival at Landsberg, Hitler found he was treated as something of a celebrity. His cell door was left open most of the time, he had the freedom of the prison grounds, and he could receive visitors. It was during this period of incarceration that Hitler wrote the first part of his book; Mein Kampf (My Struggle). His friend and fellow-prisoner, Rudolf Hess, acted as secretary to Hitler during this time.

Adolf Hitler was released from Landsberg Prison on 20 December 1924. He had in fact served less than twelve months of the five year sentence. Upon his release he immediately returned to Berchtesgaden where he stayed with friends and benefactors. One of the terms of Hitler's early prison release was a ban on public speaking. But that did not stop Adolf Hitler; he still found opportunities to speak to local people and those in the surrounding areas. He did however keep quite a low profile, should the authorities back in Munich get wind of his public speaking activities he might just find himself back in prison. It was during this time, while renting a small hut on the Obersalzberg above Berchtesgaden that Hitler wrote the second part of his book, Mein Kampf.

Through the following years the fortunes of the NSDAP went from strength to strength, chiefly thanks to the charismatic, almost magnetic personality and oratory of its leader, Adolf Hitler. While never able to achieve an overall majority in the Reichstag, the NSDAP achieved great electoral success during the many elections held in Germany through the late 1920s and early 1930s. The elections held in November 1932 saw the Nazis emerge as the single strongest political party in Germany. In the end the NSDAP came to power by legal means. No longer able to exclude Hitler and the Nazis from power, Franz von Papen, the German Chancellor, and Field Marshal Paul von Hindenburg, the ageing German President, did a deal, they offered Hitler the Chancellorship, believing in this way they might contain and control him. They were wrong. Once in power, Hitler, the skilled politician, easily outmanoeuvred his soon to be bewildered would-be keepers with ease.

Adolf Hitler acted quickly in his bid to gather all power unto himself. The Enabling Act which was passed on 24 March 1933 gave him independence from both the Reichstag and the President. Previous Chancellors had been dependent on the President's power to issue emergency decrees under Article 48 of the Constitution. Hitler now reserved that right for himself; furthermore he now had the right to set aside the Constitution itself. President von Hindenburg died on 2 August 1934. Within a matter of hours of his passing it was announced that henceforth the office of President would be merged with that of Chancellor. Effectively Adolf Hitler would become Head of State and Commander-in-Chief of the German Armed Forces. Later that day the men of the German Army took the oath of allegiance to their new commander, Adolf Hitler.

On 19 August 1934 the German people went to the polls to express their opinions regarding Hitler's amalgamating the powers of the President's office with that of his role as Reich's Chancellor. 95.7 per cent of the electorate went to the polls. Of over forty-five million voters who turned out, thirty-eight million, 89.93 per cent voted in favour. Hitler was jubilant; he had achieved everything he had set out to. The following years were spent openly defying the terms of the much-hated Versailles Treaty imposed on the German nation in 1919. Hitler set about regaining many of the former German territories lost following the First World War. Again, apart from some diplomatic protesting on the part of the Western Allies, chiefly Britain and France, there was no action taken. Even when German forces entered Czechoslovakia in 1939 the European powers sat idly by. Hitler's popularity at home was now immense. German national pride had been restored. The injustices of the Versailles Treaty had been redressed.

The Führer would soon turn his attention towards Poland and the east, leading his reinvigorated country into a world war that that would spell disaster for millions. Adolf Hitler would shoot himself in his Berlin bunker on 30 April 1945 as the great empire he had built crumbled around him. Eva Hitler would take cyanide. The Führer had left instructions as to what should take place after his death, and these were followed to the letter. Hitler had previously ordered that fuel should be collected and brought to the Reich's Chancellery. The two bodies were carried up out of the bunker, then, under almost continuous Russian artillery bombardment, the remains were placed side by side in a shell crater close to the bunker entrance. Fuel was poured into the crater and over the remains, then set alight.

Baldur von Schirach

Baldur Benedikt von Schirach was born in Berlin on 9 March 1907. His father, Carl, had been an officer in the Garde-Kürassier-Regiment Wilhelm II until 1908, when he left the army to become a theatre director. Baldur von Schirach began studying Germanic folklore and art history in Munich in 1924. It was there that he fell in with a group of National Socialists. Finding that the views of this group were very similar to his own views von Schirach joined the NSDAP in 1925. He was active in recruiting students to the Nazi movement and in 1931 he was appointed *Reishsjugendführer der NSDAP* (Reich Youth Leader of the NSDAP). A law enacted on 1 December 1936 made the Hitler Youth the only legal organization open to German youth aged ten to eighteen years. Hitler

151. Reich's Governor Baldur v. Schirach.
Baldur Benedikt von Schirach, Head of the Hitler Youth and later *Gauleiter* (District Leader) of Vienna.

decreed that all German youth must become members of this new youth organization. By the end of 1938 the Hitler Youth had about eight million members. That said, a large number of German children managed to avoid becoming members despite the risk of fines and possible imprisonment to their parents.

As Head of the Hitler Youth von Schirach oversaw the introduction of the indoctrination programmes designed to influence young people throughout the Reich. Von Schirach married Henriette Hoffmann, the daughter of Heinrich Hoffmann, Hitler's personal photographer on 31 March 1932. The couple were members of the Führer's inner circle; as such they were often Hitler's guests at his private residence the Berghof on the Obersalzberg. The von Schirachs had four children, one daughter and three sons, born between 1933 and 1942.

Baldur von Schirach organized the evacuation of many thousands of children from German cities in the face of anticipated Allied bombing. In early 1940 von Schirach volunteered. He joined the army and saw service on the Western Front where he won the Iron Cross. The fall of France in June 1940 and a reduction in the fighting in the West saw von Schirach recalled to Berlin. Hitler feared that von Schirach might become too powerful if he returned to his former post as head of the Hitler Youth. As a result Hitler appointed von Schirach *Gauleiter* (District Leader) of Vienna. Artur Axmann succeeded von Schirach as Hitler Youth leader.

As *Gauleiter* of Vienna, von Schirach oversaw the transportation of some 65,000 Jews from the city to the concentration camps in Poland. In 1943 his wife Henriette visited the Netherlands. While in Amsterdam she witnessed the rounding up of Jews in the city. Absolutely horrified, she was determined to bring the matter to Hitler's attention at their next meeting. On visiting the Berghof soon after, Henriette von Schirach, perhaps unwisely, tentatively touched on the subject with Hitler. The Führer fell silent. Henriette continued, describing what she had seen. Hitler flew into a rage, he told her not to pursue the subject. This created a terrible atmosphere in the room, no-one knowing what to say. The von Schirachs made their excuses and left the Berghof. This incident led to a breakdown in the relationship between the Führer and the von Schirachs.

Baldur von Schirach remained *Gauleiter* of Vienna until the end of the Second World War. He was tried at Nürnberg and sentenced to twenty years imprisonment. He was released together with Albert Speer on 30 September 1966. Their release would leave Rudolf Hess alone, the last of the Nazi leadership to remain in Berlin's Spandau Prison. Baldur von Schirach died at Kröv, a town in the Rhineland on 8 August 1974. His wife Henriette divorced him while he was in prison in 1946. She died on 27 January 1992.

Albert Speer

Berthold Konrad Hermann Albert Speer was born in Mannheim on 19 March 1905. His father, also Albert, was an architect. Under pressure from his father, the young Speer gave up his wish to study mathematics and instead followed family tradition to study architecture. Through the 1920s Speer studied in Karlsruhe, Munich and Berlin. On passing his exams in 1927 Albert Speer worked as assistant to Professor Heinrich

152. Professor Speer.
Berthold Konrad Hermann Albert Speer, Hitler's favourite architect and later Reich Minister for Armaments and War Production.

Tessenow from 1927 until 1930. Speer, who had previously shown little interest in politics, encouraged by some of his students attended a political meeting in Berlin in late 1930. There he would hear Adolf Hitler speak for the first time. The meeting hall was packed with students and the young architect came away much impressed by Hitler. Albert Speer joined the Nazi Party soon after.

Despite family opposition, Albert Speer married Margarete Weber on 28 August 1928 in Berlin. Speer's mother, Luise, in particular, disapproved of his choice believing his wife's family were of a lower class. The couple would have six children. However in early 1931 financial constraints led to the young architect losing his job. Speer, now unemployed began looking for work. Fortunately for him, Speer had contacts within the NSDAP. He was offered work renovating the Party's office building in Berlin. Soon after the Nazis came to power in 1933, Joseph Goebbels commissioned Speer to renovate his own Propaganda Ministry building on Berlin's Wilhelmplatz.

Speer was later commissioned to submit designs for the Nürnberg Stadium. This led to a first meeting with Adolf Hitler. Many such meetings followed. Hitler warmed to the young architect. It has been said that perhaps Hitler saw many of his own youthful aspirations reflected in Albert Speer. The Führer, himself something of a frustrated architect, admired and respected Speer for his flair, skill and imagination. Speer soon became one of Hitler's inner circle. The Führer would describe Speer as a 'kindred spirit'. The young architect was invited to live on the Obersalzberg above Berchtesgaden. Speer designed and constructed his own studio close to his new home on the Obersalzberg. Hitler and Speer would spend many hours discussing plans and building projects in the studio during Hitler's numerous impromptu visits where the Führer often presented his own sketches and drawings.

In 1934 Albert Speer received his most important commission to date. The Führer asked Speer to design and construct a complex of huge structures for the Party Rally Grounds in Nürnberg. These structures have already been covered in depth on previous pages. Hitler was extremely pleased with Speer's work at Nürnberg and at the beginning of 1937 Hitler told Speer of his plans for the remodelling and rebuilding of Berlin. Berlin was to be renamed Germania. As such it would be the new capital of Hitler's planned 'Thousand Year Reich'. In 1938 Hitler instructed Speer to construct a new Reich's Chancellery in Berlin. Speer had just one year to complete the task. The project was completed on time. Hitler was impressed and absolutely delighted with the new Chancellery. In recognition, the Führer awarded Speer the Nazi Golden Party Badge in appreciation of his work on the Chancellery.

Professor Paul Ludwig Troost, allegedly Hitler's favourite architect died on 21 January 1934. Albert Speer, friend and confidant of the Führer succeeded Troost. Speer could do no wrong in Hitler's eyes. When on 8 February 1942, Dr Fritz Todt, Minister for Armaments and Munitions was killed in a plane crash on leaving the Wolf's Lair, the Führer's eastern headquarters near Rastenburg in East Prussia, it was to Speer that Hitler turned, appointing him Todt's successor. Albert Speer proved more than equal to the task. Production increased across the board reaching its high point in 1944, despite the damage inflicted on German industry by Allied bombing. Speer's 'central planning programme' certainly enabled Germany to continue the war for much longer than would otherwise have been possible. In the final months of the Second World War it was Speer and Goebbels who were seen in public attempting to maintain morale and inspire the people. Virtually without exception these two men were the only members of the Nazi hierarchy then to be seen in public.

Speer's last meeting with Hitler was on 20 April 1945 in the Berlin bunker. He came to celebrate the Führer's fifty-sixth birthday. Albert Speer said goodbye to Adolf Hitler for the last time as he left the bunker early on the morning of 24 April 1945. Speer was captured by the Allies and stood trial at Nürnberg. He was sentenced to twenty years imprisonment. Speer was released with Baldur von Schirach in 1966, the last two Nazi prisoners to be released from Spandau Prison. On his release Speer returned to his home town of Heidelberg where he spent the remainder of his life writing. In 1981 Speer travelled in England to take part in a television programme with the BBC. Albert Speer died in London on 1 September 1981 following a heart attack. He is buried in Heidelberg, Germany.

Julius Streicher

It would be difficult when writing about the Nuremberg Rallies not to say more about Julius Streicher, the ardent anti-Semite and once Nazi *Gauleiter* (District Leader) of the city of Nuremberg. Streicher's control and influence in Nuremberg would play a part in the decision to hold the annual *Reichsparteitage* in the city during the 1930s. Julius Streicher was born in the Bavarian village of Fleinhausen west of Augsburg on 12 February 1885. His father, Friedrich, was a teacher in a Roman Catholic primary school. Julius was the last of nine children born to Friedrich and Anna Streicher. In 1909, aged twenty-four, Julius Streicher began a career as a teacher in a suburb of Nuremberg. In 1911 Streicher joined the German Democratic Party, and thus began his interest in politics.

Streicher married Kunigunde Roth, a Nuremberg baker's daughter in 1913. Their first son, Lothar was born in 1915, a second son, Elmar, was born in 1918. Julius Streicher joined the German Army at the outbreak of the First World War in 1914. Initially serving as a lance-corporal with a Bavarian infantry regiment Streicher would go on to win the Iron Cross both First and Second Class during the conflict. When the Armistice was signed in 1918 Julius Streicher was a lieutenant in a machine-gun unit. He left the army in 1918. Streicher returned to teaching and began to play an active role in right-wing politics. In 1919 he joined the *Deutschvölkischer Schutz-und-Trutz Bund* (German Nationalist Protection and Defence Federation) where he was particularly active. Streicher believed the Jews responsible for Germany's defeat in 1918. [Later, during his testimony before the International Military Tribunal at Nuremberg in 1946, Streicher stated; *'In the November revolution of 1918 the Jews and their friends had seized the political power in Germany. Jews were in the Reich Cabinet and in all the provincial governments.'*]

In 1920 Julius Streicher formed his own political party, the *Deutschsozialistische Partei* (German Socialist Party) a party based exclusively on anti-Semitism. It was by pure chance that someone suggested to Streicher that he should hear Adolf Hitler speak; and so in 1921 Streicher attended a Nazi Party meeting in the Bürgerbräu Keller in Munich. Streicher later stated: *'I experienced something which transcended the commonplace. When he finished his speech, an inner voice bade me get up. I went to the platform. When Adolf Hitler came down, I approached him and told him my name.'* This meeting

153. Julius Streicher.
This Hoffmann posed studio postcard image shows Streicher wearing the Iron Cross First Class that he won during the First World War. A gold Nazi Party Badge is attached to his tie.

transformed Julius Streicher. In 1922 he joined the Nazi Party and soon merged the entire membership of his own party with the Nazis. This single, and somewhat calculated act, almost doubled the number of Nazi Party members overnight. Hitler, for his part, would never forget what Streicher had done. Hitler would thereafter always defend Streicher by way of recognition of his loyalty.

In April 1923 Julius Streicher founded *Der Stürmer* (The Stormer/The Attacker) an illustrated weekly newspaper. *Der Stürmer* would quickly gain a reputation as Germany's most virulent anti-Semitic paper. That same year Streicher wrote an article in which he absolutely condemned inter-racial breeding. This was particularly aimed at the French who deliberately stationed Negro soldiers in the Rhineland region. Streicher wrote: 'When a Negro soldier on the Rhine misuses a German girl, she is lost to the race.' On 9 November 1923 Streicher marched beside Hitler during the failed Munich Beer-Hall *Putsch* (Revolt). Again this act of unflinching loyalty further earned Hitler's trust. Streicher, for his part in the *Putsch,* was sentenced to one month in prison.

The Nazi Party was declared an illegal organization, but it would continue in an underground form through the period of the ban until re-established and re-organized in 1925. In 1925 Streicher was appointed NSDAP *Gauleiter* of Franconia, with headquarters in Nuremberg. At that time the *Gauleiters* were merely party organizers in their respective areas with little real power. However following the seizure of power in 1933 the *Gauleiters* would become extremely powerful.

During a speech in Nuremberg in April 1925 Streicher said: 'You must realize that the Jew wants our people to perish. That is why you must join us and leave those who have brought you nothing but war, inflation, and discord. For thousands of years the Jew has been destroying the nations.' Julius Streicher was finally dismissed from his teaching post in 1928, chiefly for insisting that his pupils greet him with the term 'Heil Hitler' when he entered the classroom.

Adolf Hitler was himself an avid reader of *Der Stürmer.* Indeed the Führer stated it was his favourite newspaper. Copies of *Der Stürmer* were posted in specially constructed glazed display cases for public reading. The paper achieved an 800,000 circulation peak in 1938. Julius Streicher was elected to the Reichstag in January 1933 as Nazi delegate from Thuringia. Streicher strongly supported the Nuremberg Laws on citizenship and race introduced in 1935. That same year Martin Bormann sent a letter to every *Gauleiter* stating that *Der Stürmer* was not a Party publication, nor was it connected to the Party in any way. This was taken by some *Gauleiters* as an instruction neither to order nor to display copies of the newspaper in their district. Despite Hitler's continued support, Streicher's fall from grace was underway.

Streicher added to his own demise when he stated that Hermann Göring's daughter Edda, had not been conceived naturally, but had been conceived by artificial insemination. It was not wise to incur the wrath of the Reichsmarshall; while Streicher retracted the accusation, Göring remained furious. This would eventually force Hitler to place a speaking ban on Streicher; nonetheless Hitler and Streicher remained on good terms. Furthermore, Streicher had made several scathing verbal attacks on other *Gauleiters.* This led to his making a number of enemies amongst other high-ranking Party officials. Streicher's somewhat reckless ambition and disagreeable temperament led to numerous accusations, predominately that of profiteering. In February 1940 Streicher stood trial in Nuremberg on charges of corruption. A vengeful Göring had appointed a commission to look into Streicher's business transactions and even his personal life that same year. At the end of the proceedings Julius Streicher was forced to resign as *Gauleiter* of Franconia, stripped of his Party posts, and, subject to what amounted to virtual house arrest he was banished to his country estate. He was however, under Hitler's instructions, permitted to continue to contribute to, and to publish *Der Stürmer*. The last issue of the paper appeared in late February 1945.

Streicher's wife Kunigunde died in 1943. As the Second World War reached its inevitable conclusion Julius Streicher married his secretary of five years, Adele Tappe on 20 May 1945. He was captured by American forces three days later on 23 May 1945 in Waidring in Austria. Julius Streicher was tried on a charge of 'crimes against humanity' as a result of his inflammatory writings and numerous speeches over some twenty-five years. During the trials Streicher claimed to have been beaten and tortured by his American prison guards. Rightly or wrongly his claims were not investigated and remained ignored. He was sentenced to death on 1 October 1946. Streicher was hanged early on the morning of 16 October 1946. As he reached the bottom of the scaffold Streicher shouted: '*Heil Hitler!*'

Acknowledgements

There are those who deserve a great deal of thanks for their kind assistance and indulgence while I was carrying out the research and planning for this book.

David and Christine Harper, Eagle's Nest Historical Tours, Kurdirektion, Berchtesgaden, for their tolerance and kindness during the period that I worked with them as tour guide through the 2009/2010 seasons; a delightful experience that I hope to repeat at some point in the future.

All at Pen & Sword Books Limited for their continued support.

The **Bayerische Staatsbibliothek München/Fotoarchiv Hoffmann**, now own part of the Heinrich Hoffmann Picture Archive, including the reproduction rights to those images in their possession. A number of images appearing in *'The Nazis' Nuremberg Rallies'*, belong to the **Bayerische Staatsbibliothek München/Fotoarchiv Hoffmann**.

Finally, Lena, for having endured further hours of neglect while I was absorbed on this latest project.

Bibliography

The following is a list of books that have proved useful in the preparation of this work.

Bullock, Alan, *Hitler a Study in Tyranny,* C. Tinling & Co. Ltd., 1954.
    Originally published by Odhams Press Ltd.
Evans, Richard J, *The Coming of the Third Reich,* Penguin Books, 2003.
Evans, Richard J, *The Third Reich in Power,* Penguin Books, 2005.
Shirer, William L, *The Rise and Fall of the Third Reich,* Pan Books Ltd., 1964.
    First published by Secker & Warburg, 1960.
Snyder, Louis L, *Encyclopaedia of the Third Reich,* The Promotional Reprint Company
    Ltd., 1995.
Toland, John, *Adolf Hitler,* Ballantine Books, 1977.

164

Appendix

The following information has been taken from the reverse of the postcards shown throughout this book (together with dates of postmarks where these exist). It is offered by way of acknowledgment and credit to the original photographers and publishers of these postcard images. This information may be referenced by using the corresponding number which relates to each postcard caption.

The reverse of some of the more interesting postcards are also shown on these pages.

1. Reverse unmarked, source unknown.
2. Herausgegeben von der N.S. Volkswohlfahrt. Photo: Heinrich Hoffmann, München.
3. Reverse unmarked, source unknown.
4. Photograph by author.
5. Verlag Frz. Eher Nachf., München 2RO / Kupsertiesdruck Brend'amour, Simhart & Co., München. Posted: 1.9.1933.
6. Reverse unmarked, source unknown. Posted: 18.4.1933.
7. Kunst und Kalenderverlag GmbH., Nürnberg.
8. Günther, Kirstein & Wendler, Leipzig O 27.
9. Echte Photographie.
10. Reverse unmarked, source unknown. Posted: 24.2.1941.
11. Kunstverlag Georg Michel, Nürnberg. Posted: 25.9.1944.
12. Verlag: Zweckverband Reichsparteitag Nürnberg. Aufnahme: Kurt Grimm. Echte Photographie.
13. Photo: Hoffmann, München, Theresienstraße 74.
14. Der Reichs-Bildberichterstatter der NSDAP., Heinrich Hoffmann.
15. Echte Photographie.
16. Der Reichs-Bildberichterstatter der NSDAP., Heinrich Hoffmann.
17. Best.-Nr. A/1.
18. Der Reichs-Bildberichterstatter der NSDAP., Heinrich Hoffmann.
19. Photo-Hoffmann, Berlin SW68, Kochstr.10.
20. Der Reichs-Bildberichterstatter der NSDAP., Heinrich Hoffmann.
21. Der Reichs-Bildberichterstatter der NSDAP., Heinrich Hoffmann.
22. Verlag Frz. Eher Nachf., München 2RO / Kupsertiesdruck Brend'amour, Simhart & Co., München.
23. Verlag: Liebermann & Co., Nürnberg-W. Echte Photographie.
24. Karl Kolb, Nürnberg, Tafelfeldstr. 34. Ruf: 42647.
25. Reverse unmarked, source unknown.
26. Verlag: Ludwig Riffelmacher, Fürth i. Bayern, Würzburger Straße 201. Rila-Karte.
27. Stoja-Verlag Paul Janke, Nürnberg-A. Orginalabzug aus den Photo-Werkstätten Stojaverlag-Nürnberg.
28. Stoja-Verlag Paul Janke, Nürnberg-A. Posted: 21.6.1943.

29. Herstellung und Verlag: Graphische Kunstanstalt Zerreiss & Co., Nürnberg.
30. Verlag F. Willmy, Nürnberg. Posted: 5.9.34.
31. Herstellung und Verlag: Graphische Kunstanstalt Zerreiss & Co., Nürnberg. Photo: Kurt Grimm, Nbg.
32. Reverse unmarked, source unknown. Posted: 4.9.1944.
33. Verlag und Eigentumsrecht Liebermann & Co. Nürnberg. Freig. d. R.L.M. vom 24.9.36.
34. Stoja-Verlag Paul Janke, Nürnberg-N. Echte Photographie.
35. Driesen Postkarten-Verlag Berlin N 58.
36. Privately taken photograph. Reverse unmarked, source unknown.
37. Privately taken photograph. Reverse unmarked, source unknown.
38. Privately taken photograph. Reverse unmarked, source unknown.
39. Privately taken photograph. Reverse unmarked, source unknown.
40. Privately taken photograph. Reverse unmarked, source unknown.
41. Photograph by author.
42. Privately taken photograph. Reverse unmarked, source unknown.
43. Photograph by author.
44. Ludwig Harren, Allersbergerstr. 4, Nürnberg-O. Nur Allersbergerstr. 4.
45. Photo-Hoffmann, München, Theresienstr. 74. Echte Fotografie.

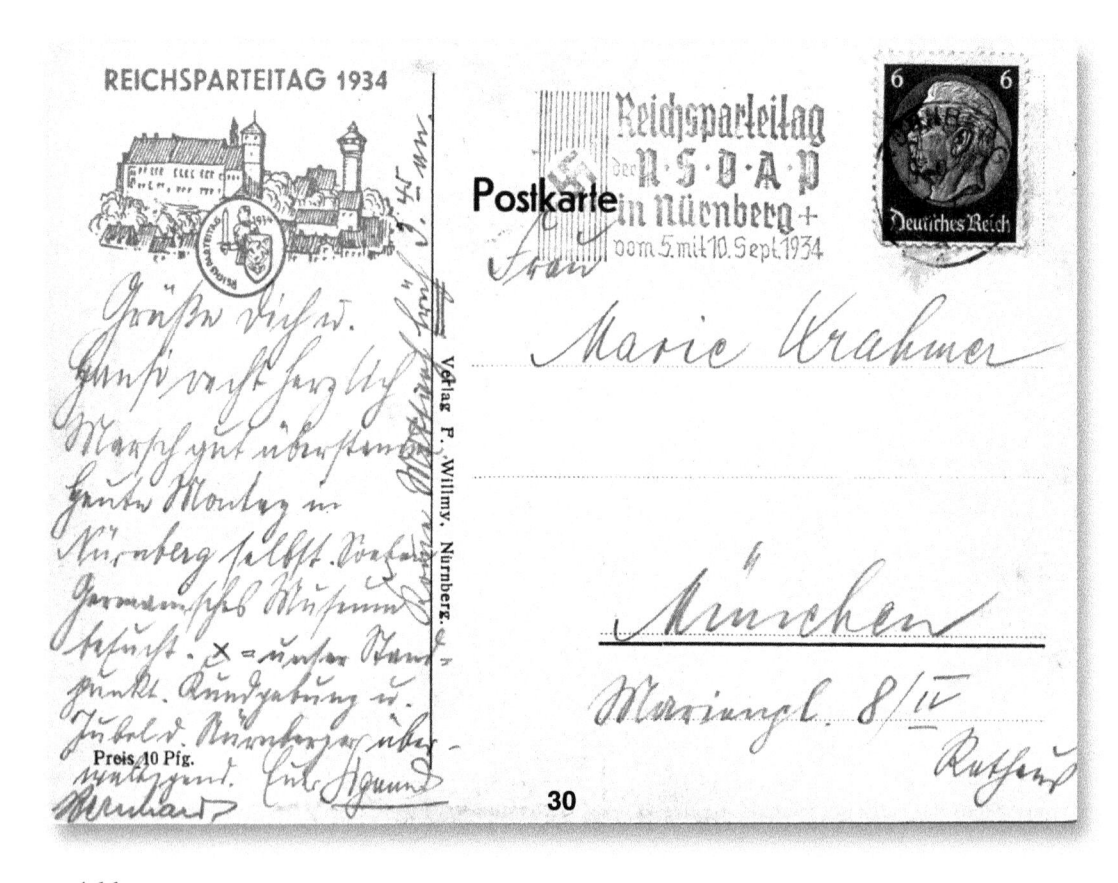

47

46. Verlag Frz. Eher Nachf., München 2 RO / Kupsertiesdruck Brend'amour, Simhart & Co., München.
47. Verlag Frz. Eher Nachf., München 2 RO / Kupsertiesdruck Brend'amour, Simhart & Co., München. Posted: 14.9.35.
48. Stoja-Verlag Paul Janke, Nürnberg-A. Orginalabzug aus den Photo-Werkstätten Stojaverlag-Nürnberg.
49. Der Reichs-Bildberichterstatter der NSDAP., Heinrich Hoffmann.
50. Verlag Intra, Nürnberg.
51. Der Reichs-Bildberichterstatter der NSDAP., Heinrich Hoffmann.
52. Der Reichs-Bildberichterstatter der NSDAP., Heinrich Hoffmann.
53. Verlag Intra, Nürnberg.
54. Herstellung und Verlag: Graphische Kunstanstalt Zerreiss & Co., Nürnberg.
55. Der Reichs-Bildberichterstatter der NSDAP., Heinrich Hoffmann.
56. Der Reichs-Bildberichterstatter der NSDAP., Heinrich Hoffmann.
57. Reverse unmarked, source unknown.
58. Der Reichs-Bildberichterstatter der NSDAP., Heinrich Hoffmann.
59. Der Reichs-Bildberichterstatter der NSDAP., Heinrich Hoffmann.
60. Der Reichs-Bildberichterstatter der NSDAP., Heinrich Hoffmann.
61. Karl Kolb, Nürnberg, Tafelfeldstr. 34. Ruf: 42647.
62. Der Reichs-Bildberichterstatter der NSDAP., Heinrich Hoffmann.

63. Der Reichs-Bildberichterstatter der NSDAP., Heinrich Hoffmann.
64. Der Reichs-Bildberichterstatter der NSDAP., Heinrich Hoffmann.
65. Photo-Hoffmann, München, Theresienstr. 74. Echte Photographie.
66. Karl Kolb, Nürnberg, Tafelfeldstr. 34. Ruf: 42647.
67. Photo: Kurt Grimm – Verlag: Bruno Panzer, Nürnberg, Tucherstraße 2 – Zeder-Druck.
68. Zentralverlag der NSDAP. Franz Eher Nachfolger, München. Posted: 9.9.36.
69. Zentralverlag der NSDAP. Frz. Eher Nachf., München. Druck: Brend'amour, Simhart & Co., München.
70. Reverse unmarked, source unknown.
71. Verlag u. Eigentumsrecht Liebermann & Co. Nürnberg. Echte Fotografie.
72. Photograph by author.
73. Verlag: Mischler Schleyer, Nürnberg, Königstr. 2a. Posted: 27.8.42.
74. Photograph by author.
75. Reverse unmarked, source unknown.
76. Bromsilber-Imitation.
77. Reverse unmarked, source unknown. Posted: 10.9.1936.
78. Verlag Intra Nürnberg. Druck: Noris-Verlag G.m.b.H., Nürnberg.
79. Photo Harren, Färberstrasse und Allersbergerstr. Nürnberg.
80. Karl Kolb, Nürnberg, Tafelfeldstr. 34. Ruf: 42647.
81. Verlag von Ludwig Riffelmacher, Fürth i. Bayern, Würzburgerstr. 201. Hansa Luftbild München. Freigegeben d. R.L.M. Echte Photographie Rila-Karte.

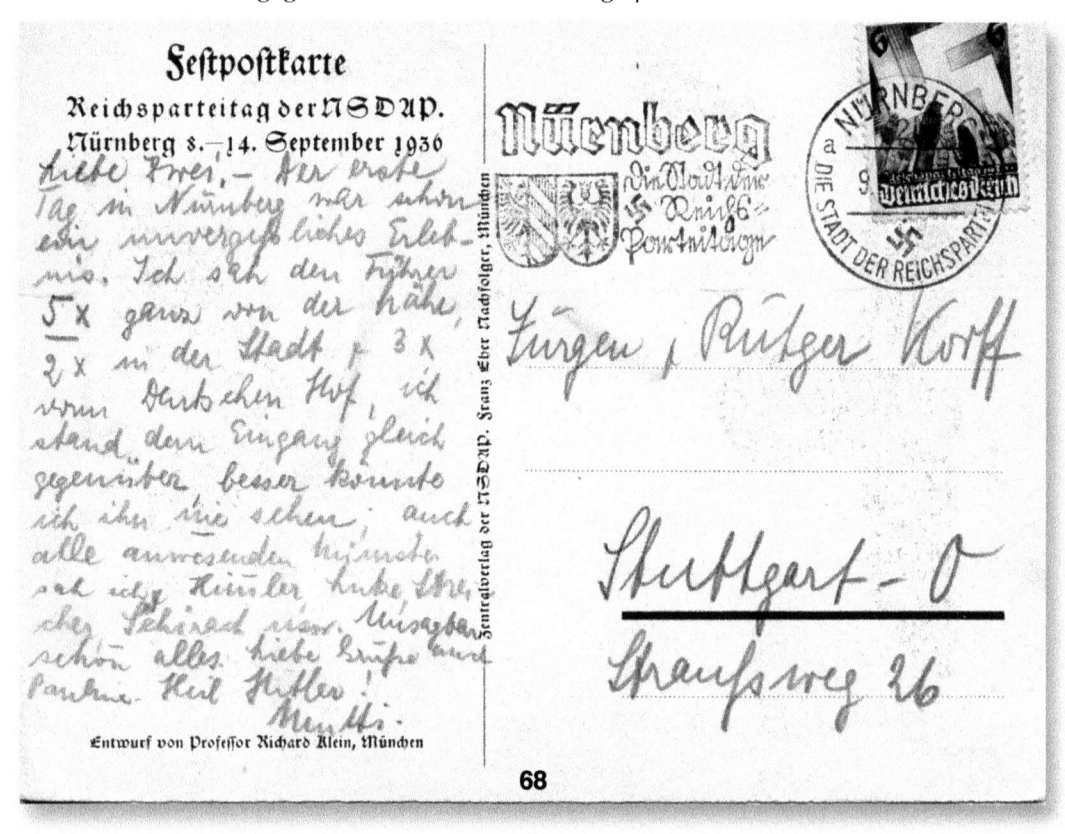

68

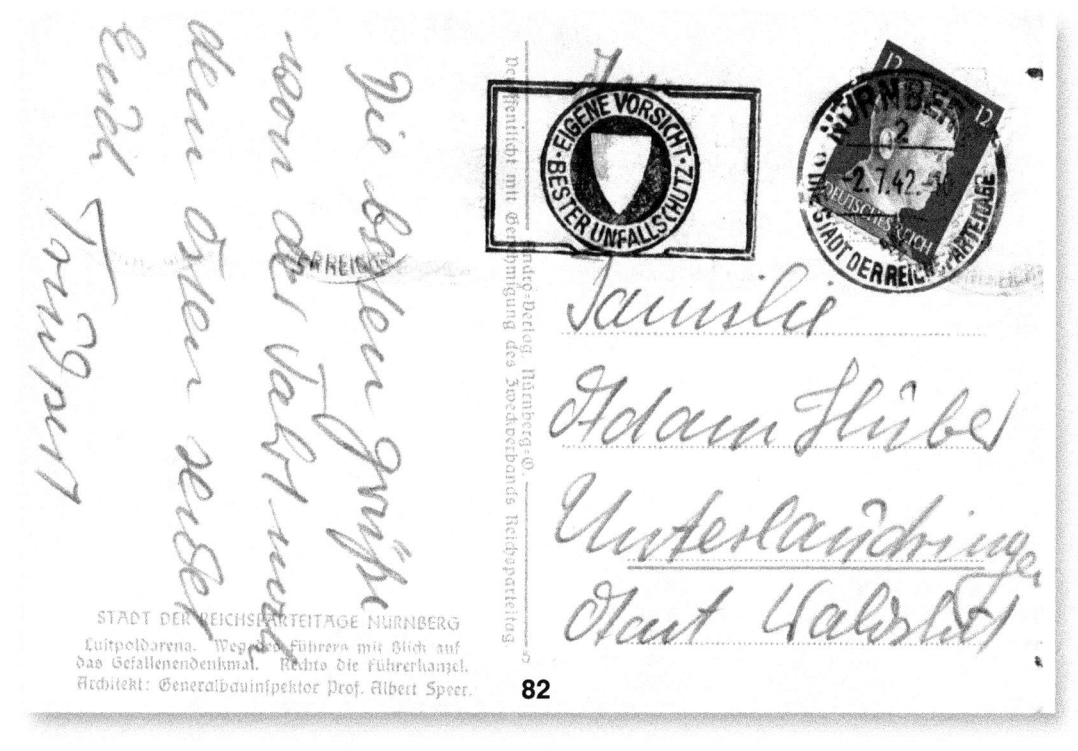

82. Andro-Verlag, München-O. Veröffentlicht mit Genehmigung des Zweckverbands Reichsparteitag. Posted: 2.7.1942.
83. Verlag Intra Nürnberg. Druck: Noris-Verlag G.m.b.H., Nürnberg. Posted: 17.9.36.
84. Photo: Hoffmann, München, Theresienstraße 74.
85. Verlag Intra Nürnberg.
86. Industrie-Fotografen Klinke & Co., Berlin W8, Leipziger Str. 24. Fliegeraufnahme. Freggegeben durch R.L.M. Echtes Foto.
87. Stoja-Verlag Paul Janke, Nürnberg-A.
88. Aufnahme: Kurt Grimm, Nürnberg. Andro-Verlag, Nürnberg-O. Echte Photographie.
89. Aufnahme: Kurt Grimm, Nürnberg. Andro-Verlag, Nürnberg-O. Echte Photographie.
90. Photograph by author.
91. Photograph by author.
92. Zentralverlag der NSDAP., Frz. Eher Nachf., München – Druck: Mandruck A.G., München. Commemorative postmark dated: 13.9.1927.
93. Zentralverlag der NSDAP. Frz. Eher Nachf., München. Commemorative postmark dated: 10.9.1937. Druck: Brend'amour, Simhart & Co., München.
94. Herstellung und Verlag: Graphische Kunstanstalt Zerreiss & Co., Nürnberg. Posted: 12.9.1937.
95. Druck und Verlag: Universum-Verlagsanstalt G.m.b.H., Berlin-Tempelhof. Aufn: Karl Kolb, Nürnberg.
96. Photo-Hoffmann, München, Theresienstraße 74. Posted: 9.9.37.
97. Herstellung und Verlag: Graphische Kunstanstalt Zerreiss & Co., Nürnberg. Posted: 11.9.37.

98. Verlag Intra Nürnberg. Druck: Noris-Verlag G.m.b.H., Nürnberg.
99. Herstellung und Verlag: Graphische Kunstanstalt Zerreiss & Co., Nürnberg. Posted: 8.9.37.
100. Verlag: Bruno Panzer, Nürnberg, Tucherstraße 2 – Jeder-Druck. Posted: 25.9.1937.
101. Echte Photographie.
102. Verlag von Ludwig Riffelmacher, Unterfarrnbach über Fürth i. Bay. Echte Photographie.
103. Verlag von Ludwig Riffelmacher, Fürth i. Bayern, Würzburgerstr. 201. Hansa Luftbild München. Freigegeben d. R.L.M. Echte Photographie Rila-Karte.
104. Photo Harren, Färberstrasse und Allersbergerstr. Nürnberg.
105. Stoja-Verlag Paul Janke, Nürnberg-A. Aufgenommen mit Meyer Plasmat-Optik. Posted: 18.6.1943.
106. Photograph by author.
107. Stoja-Verlag Janke & Dr. Maiwald, Nürnberg-A. Orginalabzug aus den Photo-Werkstätten Stojaverlag-Nürnberg. Aufgenommen mit Meyer-Optik.
108. Photo Harren, Färberstrasse und Allersbergerstr. Nürnberg.
109. Photograph by author.
110. Stoja-Verlag Paul Janke, Nürnberg-A.
111. Stoja-Verlag Paul Janke, Nürnberg-A. Aufgenommen mit Meyer Plasmat-Optik.

105

112. Photo-Hoffmann, München, Theresienstraße 74.
113. Urheberrecht: Druck und Werbehaus K Erich Otto, Chemnitz. Verlag für die Ostmark. Verlag für Kultur und Wirtschaftswerbung, Daenell & Co., Berlin. Druck: Cyliax Druck Wien. Foto: Weltbild, Berlin. Posted 31.3.1939.
114. Reverse unmarked, source unknown.
115. Andro-Verlag, Nürnberg-O.
116. Photo-Hoffmann, München, Friedrichstraße 34. Posted: 6.9.38.
117. Zentralverlag der NSDAP. Frz. Eher Nachf., München. Druck: Brend'amour, Simhart & Co., München. Commemorative postmark dated: 9.9.1938.
118. Aufnahme: Prof. Heinrich Hoffmann München.
    Otto Schönstein – Raumbild Verlag – Diessen a. Ammersee.
119. Verlag und Eigentumsrecht Liebermann & Co., Nürnberg. Posted: 8.9.1938.
120. Photograph by author.
121. Photo-Hoffmann, München, Friedrichstraße 34. Posted: 9.9.1938.
122. Photo-Hoffmann, München, Friedrichstraße 34.
123. Verlag Intra Nürnberg. Druck: F. Willmy G.m.b.H., Nürnberg. Posted: 7.9.1938.
124. Photo-Hoffmann, München, Friedrichstraße 34.
125. Photo-Hoffmann, München, Friedrichstraße 34.
126. Verlag: O. Struck, Berlin-Lichterfelde. Druck: Otto Elsner KG., Berlin.
127. Veröffentlicht mit Genehmigung des Zweckverbands Reichsparteitag.
    Andro-Verlag, Nürnberg-O. Echte Photographie, Originalabzug. Posted: 28.3.39.

128. Photo-Hoffmann, München, Friedrichstraße 34.
129. Photo: Hoffmann. Berlin. Posted: 13.9.1938.
130. Herstellung und Verlag: Graphische Kunstanstalt Zerreiss & Co., Nürnberg.
131. Photo-Hoffmann, München, Friedrichstraße 34.
132. Herstellung und Verlag: Graphische Kunstanstalt Zerreiss & Co., Nürnberg. Posted: 12.9.1938.
133. Photo-Hoffmann, München, Friedrichstraße 34.
134. Reverse unmarked, source unknown. Posted: 10.9.1938.
135. Photo-Hoffmann, München, Friedrichstraße 34.
136. Photo-Hoffmann, München, Friedrichstraße 34.
137. A.G.N. Phot. Nbg. Rosenaustr. 6.
138. Verlag: O. Struck, Berlin-Lichterfelde. Druck: Otto Elsner KG., Berlin. Foto: Weltbild. Commemorative postmark: 'Parteitag Großdeutschlands' dated: 12.9.1938. Additional postmark: 'München – Hauptstadt der Bewegung' 9.11.1923 – 9.11.1938.
139. Herstellung und Verlag: Graphische Kunstanstalt Zerreiss & Co., Nürnberg.
140. Herstellung und Verlag: Graphische Kunstanstalt Zerreiss & Co., Nürnberg.
141. Stoja-Verlag – Paul Janke, Nürnberg-A.
142. Reverse unmarked, source unknown. Printer's proof.
143. Zentralverlag der NSDAP. Frz. Eher Nachf., München.

138

151

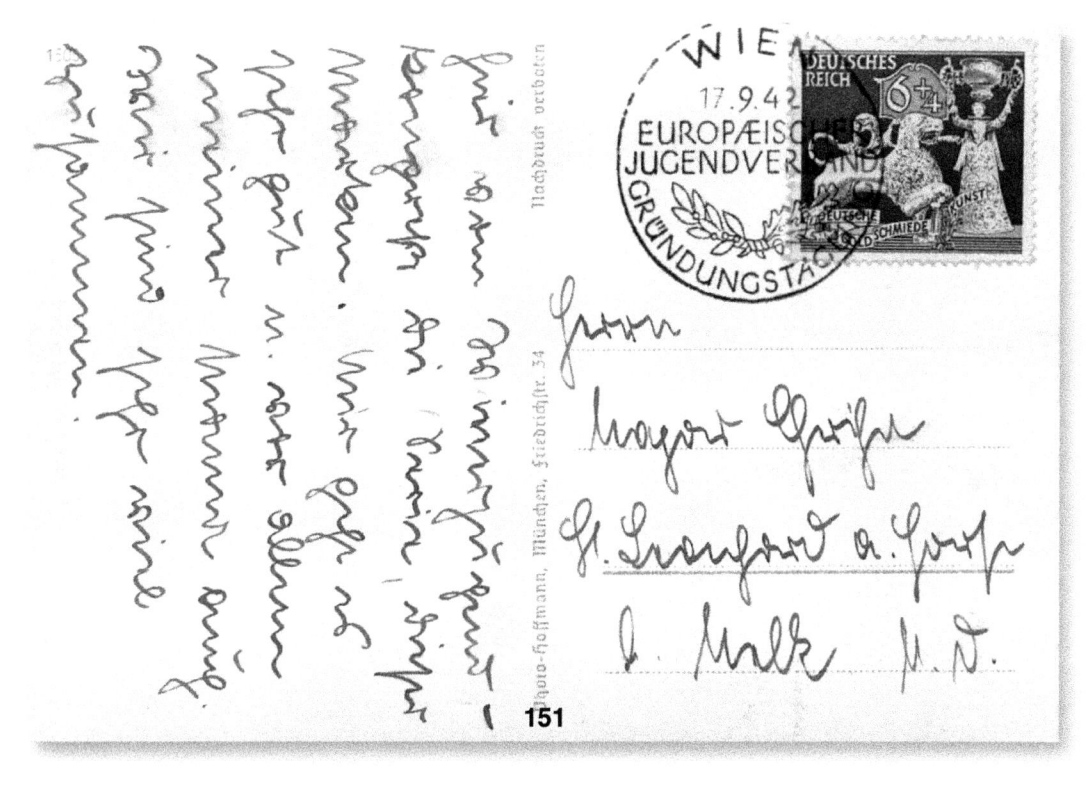

144. Reverse unmarked, source unknown. Printer's proof.
145. Der Reichs-Bildberichterstatter der NSDAP., Heinrich Hoffmann.
146. Photo-Hoffmann, München, Theresienstr. 74. Echte Fotografie.
147. Film – Foto – Verlag, Berlin SW68. Foto Rosemarie Clausen.
148. Photo-Hoffmann, München, Theresienstr. 74.
149. Contemporary official stamp on reverse reads: SS-Panzer-Grenadier-Regiment "Der Führer." Aufnahme: Fendt.
150. Photo-Hoffmann, München, Theresienstr. 74. Echte Fotografie.
151. Photo-Hoffmann, München, Friedrichstr. 34.
152. Photo-Hoffmann, München, Friedrichstr. 34. Echte Fotografie. Date stamped: 6.6.43.
153. Photo-Hoffmann, München, Theresienstr. 74.

Jacket image (front).
Main image postcard number 116.

Jacket images (back).
Postcards numbers 11 and 22. Background image postcard number 57.

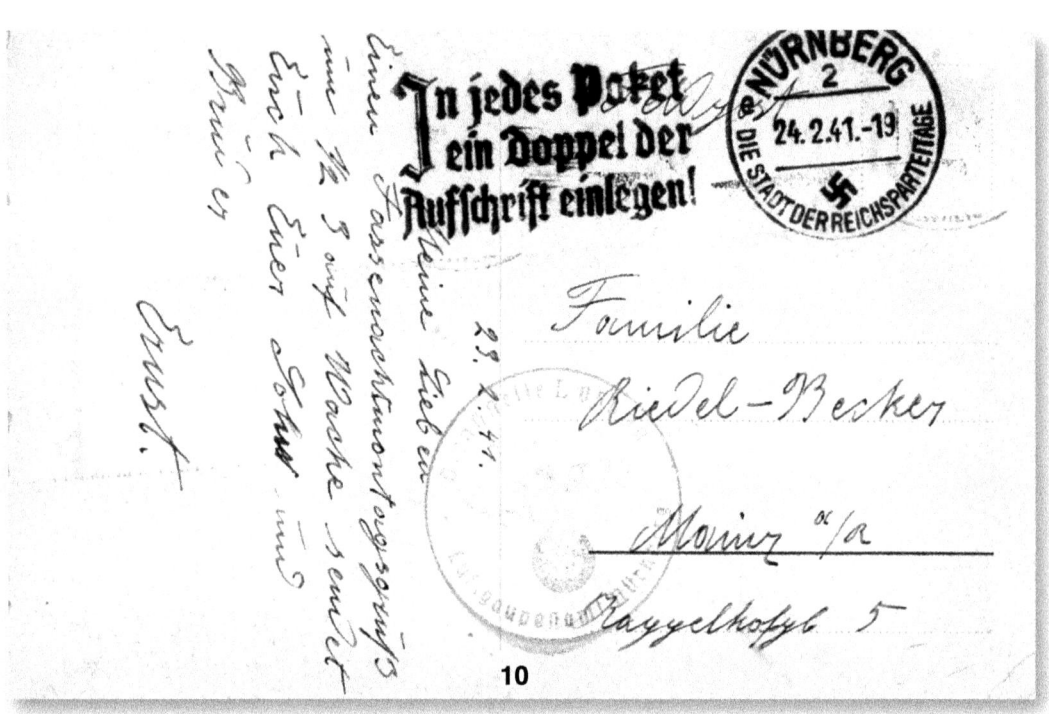

10

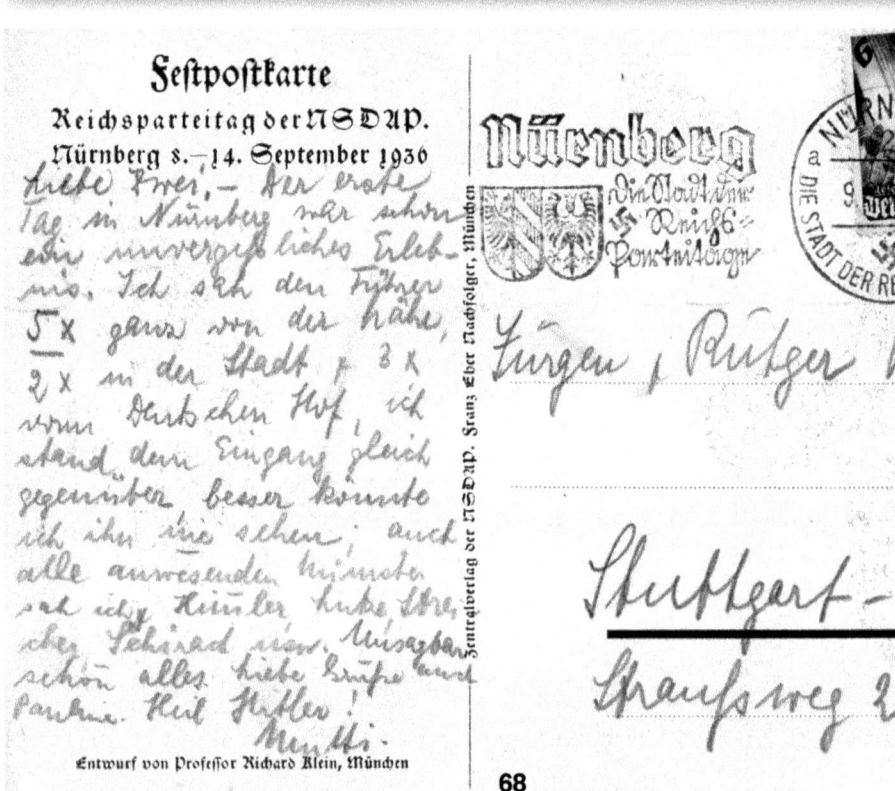

In jedes Paket / ein Doppel der / Aufschrift einlegen!

NÜRNBERG 2 / 24.2.41.-19 / DIE STADT DER REICHSPARTEITAGE

Familie
Riedel-Becker

Mainz a/R

Kaygelhofpl 5

68

Festpostkarte
Reichsparteitag der NSDAP.
Nürnberg 8.–14. September 1936

Liebe Ewer, – Der erste Tag in Nürnberg war schon ein unvergeßliches Erlebnis. Ich sah den Führer 5× ganz von der Nähe, 2× in der Stadt + 3× vom Deutschen Hof, ich stand dem Eingang gleich gegenüber, besser konnte ich ihn nie sehen; auch alle anwesenden Minister sah ich. Hitler hatte Streicher, Schirach usw. Unsagbar schön alles. Liebe Grüße und Dank. Heil Hitler!

Mutti

Entwurf von Professor Richard Klein, München

Nürnberg / Die Stadt des / Reichs- / Parteitages

NÜRNBERG / DIE STADT DER REICHSPARTEIT[AGE]

Jürgen u. Rütger Korff

Stuttgart-O

Straußweg 26